Clearing
the Way

Clearing the Way

En Route to an Ecumenical Spirituality

Gwen Cashmore and Joan Puls

WCC Publications, Geneva

Cover design: Rob Lucas

ISBN 2-8254-0980-4

© 1990 WCC Publications, World Council of Churches, 150 route de Ferney, 1211 Geneva 2, Switzerland

No. 43 in the Risk book series

Printed in Switzerland

"Go out of the gates, go out,
prepare a road for my people;
build a highway, build it up, clear away the boulders;
raise a signal to the peoples...
they shall be called a Holy People,
the Ransomed of the Lord, People long-sought,
a City not forsaken" (Isaiah 62:10, 12)

To
all who have cleared the way
for us

Table of contents

Introduction:
Clearing the Way

This book is the story of a journey, a pilgrimage. Two women, one Roman Catholic, one Anglican, have made that journey in the company of many others and as servants of the "yet to be realized" world church. This book of shared stories, of reflections, of excerpts from letters of friends around the world, is about a search to live as disciples of "one church for the one world".

It began with a chance encounter: Chicago, the Theological Institute, 1981. A conference on "Spirituality for Mission in Six Continents". Joan wasn't supposed to be there. She went as a substitute for one of the Generalate team of her Franciscan order. A few days before the event she broke her wrist (roller-skating!); she went in spite of it. Gwen happened to be in the US from Geneva. It looked like a worthwhile conference and, besides, she needed to contact Rosemary Haughton, one of the speakers. The exchange we made during that conference, and especially the ascetic accommodations, brought us together. At the end we hesitantly offered each other an address. We were both busy people with a surplus of correspondents. Perhaps we would meet again when Gwen next travelled to the USA.

The very next week Gwen saw the book, *The Go-Between God*, in a bookstall at Fuller Seminary and on an impulse bought it and sent it to Joan. The "Go-Between-God" and the theme of exchange became leit-motifs. "What causes the fellowship is the gift of awareness which opens our eyes... makes us see as we never saw before... the spark that sets off most revolution, the dangerous life-giver, the Holy Spirit."[1] Were we really on the same wave length? Yes, we were.

It was the beginning of a joint pilgrimage. After a short visit in the US six months later when Gwen was en route from Central America to Geneva, we began a joint prayer-discipline. Perhaps that was the real opening, to more than we would ever have imagined, or chosen! "Lord, I am not yet willing for you to have your way with me, but I am willing to be made willing."

In 1982 we teamed up for our first joint ministry, a Presbyterian assembly in Hartford, Connecticut. Gwen tells the story: "An unexpected invitation came to open the big Presbyterian Church of USA pre-assembly mission conference. It was a weighty task and I wanted to do it with someone. After clearing it with Joan, I told the planning group that I was willing to speak about 'signs of the kingdom' if we could *be* a sign as well, that is, do it as an Anglican-Roman Catholic team. And we did."

In 1983 things were hotting up in Geneva. Plans were well ahead for the World Council of Churches' assembly in Vancouver. Gwen was on the programme and worship committees, and, with others, anxious to ensure that the breadth of the WCC assembly was matched by its depth. She also felt it important that there should be some sign that the ecumenical movement was bigger than the WCC. Was it possible to have a continuous praying presence, a chapel open for prayer throughout the period of the assembly? Could a prayer cell led by an Anglican and a Roman Catholic, open to all who would join, precede the assembly, clear the way, so to speak? What if two people went ahead of the whole travelling circus and engaged with local people to build a praying community on the site? And so we went. "It was the creation of a tiny ecumenical prayer cell, a statement of intention that the foundation of all we were to do rested in the power and presence of God... Here (in the little St Andrew's Presbyterian chapel on the campus) prayer was held three times a day, a simple offering of liturgical prayer with intercessions for the assembly, for the church universal and for each of the 900 delegates by name."[2]

Worship was recognized as one of the highlights of the Vancouver event and spirituality became one of the themes for ongoing work. After Vancouver Gwen switched jobs and, in her new capacity as director of Renewal and Congregational Life, was given the mandate of putting some flesh on the spirituality theme! Joan's experience of renewal in her own religious community and within the US church, and her penchant for reflection and writing, were desirable resources. She became a consultant to that department and assisted in some of the research, conference planning, writing of reports, etc.

Since that joint time in Geneva, we have had ministries together in France, Yugoslavia, Canada, England, Northern and Southern Ireland, India and Germany. Our worlds began to mingle, too: Gwen meeting Joan's community in various countries, Joan's first trip to the UK. Gwen had been travelling all her life. Joan's first trip outside the US was to be with her community's Indian sisters in 1981. There were crises: Joan's bout with cancer in 1982, Gwen's financial risks after she left

Geneva, the strains of holding various worlds together (international friendships, much less international ministries, have their share of obstacles!). By 1986 Gwen had left Geneva to give full attention to working more closely with local communities. Joan had written *Every Bush is Burning*, attempting to make spirituality an everyday matter, for ordinary Christians. Gwen had long been seeking the element of "community sharing" and a life-style more compatible with values expressed by the institutions she'd served. She had a burn to be with pew people, in local areas where so many were hungering or searching, groping for their rightful roles in the *missio dei*. Joan had written in *Every Bush is Burning*: "I long for companions on my journey, a journey of holding in balance involvement and prayer, responsible action and searching reflection, the call to go abroad and the call to go deep."[3] We both became restless every time we heard or read the familiar words: "The harvest is ripe, but the labourers are few." Maybe the vast grain fields of East Anglia in the UK were a place to begin.

Withdrawing Gwen's pension money from Geneva as capital to generate a small income, we set ourselves free for a time to pray, reflect, ask questions, discern, be local. We began offering retreats, responding to invitations to facilitate local ecumenical groups, to pursue the meaning of ecumenical discipleship in our contemporary world. Joan's second book, *A Spirituality of Compassion*, fed into the exploration, as did Gwen's continued contacts with international groups. The hunger and interest were obvious. We were touching nerves that were alive. So much of the official activity of the ecumenical movement is at the level of top church leaders. Yet the pain of division and the search for unity and meaning is often felt acutely by local Christians. How can they pursue their longings for a way of living that takes seriously the prayer "that they may be one"?

Joan had until now been balancing work in Milwaukee with work in the UK. By 1989, after her third book, *Hearts Set on the Pilgrimage*, tuned in to the spirit of the current interchurch process in the UK, and Gwen had completed a substantial piece of ecumenical field-work in East Anglia, we were convinced that we were on some right tracks. We believed in being a team, in spite of the costs entailed. While team-work tempers any tendencies towards ego-trips, it demands the patience and the discipline to envision and implement together. We had times of acute tension. Joan had worked in the US in areas of spirituality and social justice. She was deeply involved in an inner-city parish in Milwaukee. She favoured questioning institutions and affirming the struggles of laity, women, the disenfranchized. Gwen felt the loss of the rich resources and opportunities that Geneva had offered. She was now experienced and at home serving on boards and committees relating to the institutional church. Free-lancing had its financial drawbacks. Writing is not a lucrative career. The strain of double residences, working together only some months of the year, showed. It was time to take a further step as a team!

We also found that we needed to be more *human* in our approach. Most of those with whom we spent time were laity, many women, and the most freeing element in our encounters was that we were human beings together, not defined by our church roles or denominational boxes. We sought a language that was not church jargon, a context that included science, poetry, literature and politics. We were pilgrims seeking a way together, a community committed to the bigness of God's purposes in our own lives and in surrounding events. "The major task of spirituality today is to humanize the structures and enlarge the common expectations of what it is to be human."[4] Or, as Donald Reeves has said, "religious questions are ecumenical questions are human questions". We described ecumenical spirituality as discipleship within a world church, the commitment to pilgrim together on behalf of the new creation.

What we lacked was a base and some assured financial support. That way opened up at last. A family house which for seventy-five years had been a centre for prayer became available to the British Council of Churches. For the last twenty-five years it had housed the Farncombe Community, committed to prayer for unity. It now needed a new direction and purpose. We were alerted and, with others, began exploring the viability of it becoming an undergirding structure for us, as well as a resource for the BCC.

It was an auspicious moment in Britain. Under the leadership of Philip Morgan, general secretary of the BCC, the "old instrument" of the ecumenical movement had offered to die so that something new might be born. Those outside the BCC, notably the Roman Catholics and black churches, joined the three-year discernment process, "Not Strangers but Pilgrims". The heart of the process is contained in this prayer:

> Lord God, we thank you for calling us into the company of those who trust in Christ and seek to obey his will. May your Spirit guide and strengthen us in mission and service to your world, for we are strangers no longer but pilgrims together on the way to your kingdom. Amen.

In the first stages of the new process, thousands of local groups were involved. That story is told elsewhere.[5] As we write, the "new instrument" is still in the labour ward.

In July 1989, we moved to Farncombe, Godalming, Surrey, appointed by the BCC as co-directors of an ecumenical spirituality project. In addition to a place and financial provision for three years, we had the support of Joan's community, a backlog of rich experiences and a faithful network of friends and fellow-seekers. Past dreams had a potential to be realized: work at the local level, work with laity, restoring a sense of the people of God, healing splits and removing blocks. In Sidney Carter's words:

> Do you believe it?
> That is not the question.
> The question is...
> What does it do to you?
> That is how you come into the story...
> What you are in
> Is not a work of art
> But total revelation.
> What you do is
> Part of the Revelation.

What prompted this book? The fact that our pilgrimage has been inextricably intertwined with the WCC and the BCC. It has been said that the ecumenical movement is people, a history of friendships. Our experiences and resulting reflections, our contacts and their influence on us, are the material out of which we write. We intend this book to be as practical and as concrete as possible. We are not proposing a theory of ecumenical spirituality. We are offering the examples, the questions, the insights, that our ecumenical journey, with others, locally and globally, has provided and prompted. In gathering our material we tapped into the rich resources of more distant friends. We asked persons in Asia, Africa, North America, Europe and Australia to reflect on several questions and to share their responses. These folks help to supply what is clearly lacking in us. We owe a debt of gratitude to all who have walked with us, as companions, co-workers, supporters, participants, critics, correspondents.

One of the joys of friendship is the opportunity to share visions and dreams. In our dreaming and longing for the right place and time to explore a joint vocation, books were often a means for us of exchange and nourishment. One such was *Hanta Yo*, a Native American novel, centred on the vision-seeking of two friends on behalf of their tribe. The title means "clear the way". Implicit in what follows is a seeking of vision with and for the people of God. Clearing the way is one preliminary essential task!

We feel that in the past eight years of our personal pilgrimage there has already been a many-levelled clearing of the way. You can imagine our reaction when we discovered that the setting for this latest phase of our ecumenical activity was a house and garden woefully cluttered and greatly in need of cleaning and clearing! If there are echoes of house-cleaning and garden-clearing in the chapters that follow, it is because they too are parables of the real task we have undertaken.

NOTES

[1] John V. Taylor, *The Go-Between God*, London, SCM, 1972, p.18.
[2] Gwen Cashmore, "The Worship of the Sixth Assembly", *Midstream*, January 1984, p.78.
[3] Joan Puls, *Every Bush is Burning*, Geneva, WCC, 1985, p.24.
[4] Source unknown.
[5] See *Views from the Pews*, Lent 1986 and local ecumenism, London, BCC, 1986.

1. What is a Global Christian? An Ecumenical Spirituality

Again and again we see a pattern of symptoms: people hungry for a bigger vision, for freedom from narrow denominational-ism, people with energy who long to belong to something which enlarges and nourishes them, and which impels them to greater practical obedience. Many people of faith can no longer bear the poverty-stricken diet their local church offers. Their inner being is ardent, their hearts are disappointed. They channel their commitments through whatever is available: Christian Aid, prayer groups, women's concerns, social justice, local issues. Many of them give up on church and put all their energies into social-political networks, even while they miss the rich under-girding that shared faith and the spiritual journey can supply.

An elder in the Church of Scotland wrote to us: "I would suggest to you that in the UK we are getting near to the position where there will be more Christians outside the church than are in it. Many like myself, although I hold on by the skin of my eyebrows, find it increasingly impossible to give credibility to the church... The church needs perestroika as much if not more than the Soviet Union."

An artist-seeker in the US has redefined church as a process. She wrote: "I am at home in the notion of church as all people seeking... If I am living right here in Holly Springs, the quality of my risk for sharing, affecting and being affected by, has a universal effect... So much of life seems to be governed by categories, which act as mental boxes of exclusion, telling us more about what we are not than what we are."

A woman in India tells us: "I find it painful to attend services at my local church. The worship is so isolated from our actual context. Prayers are said remembering trouble spots in India and in the world, but the sermons and more specifically the eucharist never point to my response as a Christian to the issue of life and death we have just prayed for. The eucharist is a ritual and the sermons speak irrelevantly of the 'goodies' of life after death."

In diverse places and under various guises, we have met that longing to belong to a universal family, to locate discipleship within the whole of God's purposes for creation, to be what we choose to call a global Christian. We have found people who know and rejoice in the connectedness of our world, in the possibilities of sharing their faith and discoveries with other Christians in other parts of the world. Many of these interestingly are people who have had direct experience outside their own cultural and religious boundaries. We have seen people challenging and feeding one another, joining in a global effort to renew and revive the dying embers of human community, wherever they are. These are people whose boats are ocean-bound. Too many others are confined within their denominational and parochial puddles.

An image we have often used is that of one of the Vancouver posters, Jesus embracing the globe. Jesus' absorbed commitment as depicted in that poster expresses a theological truth: a passionate loving of the world God made and sustains, an embrace of the totality of creation with its mix of good and evil. It is difficult to recognize in some of the rhetoric of church people that God actually loves the world and that God's redemptive purposes are for the whole of creation. Brooding on God's handiwork, the fourteenth-century Norfolk English mystic, Julian of Norwich, said it succinctly: "I saw a little thing the size of a hazel nut. And it was all that was made. God showed me three things: God made it, God loves it, God keeps it." The nature of God's being is generous, self-emptying. Let there be light. Let there be life. Nothing is too insignificant, nothing is so corrupt that it is not included within God's grasp, within the creative, redeeming, sustaining power of a merciful and just God. What has this God of gentleness and generosity, of liberation and judgment, to say to us at this time in history?

Lois Wilson, speaking in Japan in 1987, said: "To be authentically human is to centre one's life on the world God loves. It has always meant that. But today it is critical. The creation God loves is sick unto death. And the world desperately needs lovers, caretakers, gardeners, partners, who will work to preserve life rather than death, freedom rather than oppression, equality and justice rather than charity, beauty rather than ugliness... To think in this way plummets us directly into the centre of the spiritual struggle of the late twentieth century."[1] This is the central affirmation of a global Christian: that the making and breaking of human life anywhere and for whatever reason is the legitimate and necessary concern of those who follow Christ.[2] "He is the image of the invisible God. His is the primacy over all created things... The whole universe has been created through him and for him... Through him God chose to reconcile the whole universe... to reconcile all things, whether on earth or in heaven" (Col. 1:15-20).

To participate in the *missio dei* is to be a co-creator, a steward, a gardener, a lover, of the world God made and sustains. Because it is a messed up, as well as a beloved, world, global Christians are called at the same time to repent, to convert, and to struggle in solidarity with one another.

But this is not the attitude we often find among Christians in their local settings. Faithfully, once a month the Christians of a particular village in England gather. They gather across denominations and, because they believe they have a common witness, as neighbours, to the rest of the village. But the gathering is tense, and sharing, even in prayer, is limited. It is difficult to discuss real issues of concern: local sewerage problems, the delicate situation of a "traveller" family, the slow dying of the village itself. Some do not see these as within the purview of a Christian gathering. Their agenda is prayer and Bible study. For others, common prayer is shallow without commitment to the practical concerns of the village. It is difficult to even find a suitable mode of prayer for such a diverse group. Because the longing is there, the ecumenical fellowship continues, but it is weak and ineffective.

We have come up repeatedly against this dilemma, two seemingly irreconcilable theological points of view: those who see mission as participation with God in transforming the world, and those who claim that God's activity is in the church, that the world is contaminating and hostile to a Christian way of life, and that mission is primarily saving self and others from the world. This split is perhaps a basic split in Western Christianity, possibly in global Christianity. It is a split that runs through most denominations. And it is the basis for numerous other splits.

We believe and we affirm that all theology is practical theology. Our beliefs, about God and Christ and the activity of the Holy Spirit, influence our attitudes and behaviour. In Ben Weir's words: "What a time to engage in Christian mission! While we become advocates for the homeless, the unemployed, the disenfranchized and the discouraged within our own borders, we are called to look beyond our own society to the world and its needs. Faith lets you know you can't just stand back and say, I'm not here, hoping the trouble will go away. We must learn to live together."[3]

John Bell of the Iona Community describes how throughout Christ's life he tore down the barriers between what was presumed to be "of God" and what was not seen as "of God". Christian discipleship, he says, must ensure that that split is forever healed.[4] John Macquarrie spoke some years ago about the tendency of churches, ecumenical groups as well, to be introspective and segregated. How often we speak a private language, live in a world of our own, surprised that there is so little grassroots response, oblivious that we make little or no impact on the wider world. "The really dangerous and explosive divisions among people today are not (except in a very few areas) religious differences. The deep, bitter divisions that threaten the whole future of humankind run today along the lines that separate race from race, nation from nation, class from class. It is along these lines, above all, that the reconciling work of the church is desperately needed.[5]

We affirm, secondly, that all mission is God's mission. "Evangelization is mission, but mission is not merely evangelization," says Moltmann.[6] "One often speaks about 'Christian mission' or the 'church's mission'. The whole of the Bible relates to only one mission — the mission of God. All other missions have to find their place within it."[7] Mission embraces all those activities and movements that liberate (save) humanity. Where this is happening, through the power and life of the Spirit, there is church. The church is *for* the world. It is the new creation that we are building and welcoming. The church's missionary task is not primarily to draw people into itself, but to extend its embrace beyond itself. Someone has aptly said: "The church does not *have* a mission. The mission of Jesus has a church."

We are all situated in a here and now. We have a local history, work within a local community, with its specific goals and needs, its gifts and resources, its ways of worshipping and celebrating. "We all know it is the local church or group or context", wrote a friend, "which upholds and undergirds each person... No one can really grow or function without a local base and involvement. The ecumenical movement has to take the local seriously." "You are the light of the world. You are the salt of the earth." Light shines in a particular place. Salt seasons a particular meal. Each of us finds in the local community the place where our strength is used and our weakness held.

At the same time, "what happens in the microcosm of one field reflects our attitudes to the rest of our planet and beyond".[8] Each local church is inextricably bound up with the transformation of the society in which it finds itself. It is in our local contexts that we see and live with the serious effects of larger sinful structures: life strangled and life diminished. It is in our local contexts that we do or do not do battle with these death-dealing structures.

We are constantly uncovering the implications of our human relatedness. Beyond our divisions and the barriers of culture and history, we have a common calling. We sense it most poignantly perhaps during certain intense experiences: moments of breakthrough or reconciliation (the dismantling of the Berlin Wall), times of human suffering (a car-bombing or a hurricane), within the eucharistic setting. As a friend in India has said: "A worldwide church makes me part of a large family, which means I share and enjoy all its assets and gifts. Through my brothers and sisters every good in the universe becomes mine. Also the well-being of the world becomes a personal responsibility and concern, the well-being of my family."

How do we hold in creative balance the local and the global? How do we gain a view of the *world* that matches the view expressed in Ephesians of the dignity and grandeur of each human existence? How do we acquire a quality of caring that is particular, close to the earth, and that also takes into account the dispossessed throughout the earth?[9] It begins with an openness, an embrace, that exchanges prayer and love and response. Rosemary Haughton describes it thus: "Each gathered community is wholly the church, the body of Christ fully present, yet they are also linked to each other as points of exchange in that body, which includes all other churches and ultimately all created things."[10] The sin of a community, of the church, is to refuse this exchange, to be exclusive, to deny mutual vulnerability. Confessionalism, the rejection of certain aspects of life, a refusal to acknowledge the Holy Spirit's activity in other religions, exclusive claims of any kind, all deny the essential universal nature of Christ's church.

In a meeting between Rome and the WCC, Bishop Sanon of the Ivory Coast spoke of his own understanding of local and universal. He took as his starting point the community of Christians gathered around the eucharist, linked through their openness and prayer to the ancestors and to the whole church throughout the world. Our local cells, if open, reach out to the whole of creation and align themselves with the life breathed and carried by the Holy Spirit. To each cell is offered the call to go as deep into the mystery as it will. There is no limit to the potential embrace of the local community, except that set by those within it.

One US church, ministering to the poor and marginalized of a mid-western city, describes this balance of local and universal in its mission statement: "Service to and solidarity with the poor of our city and our world are central to our self-perception. Therefore, we are advocates of social justice and willingly take stands on issues within our church and our society... We are motivated to mission by our reading and understanding of the gospel... We are open to being evangelized by those to whom we minister."[11] Such a vision of church captures the three elements which we name in this book as integral to an ecumenical spirituality: openness, connectedness, and earthedness. It captures the essential nature of church as the community, the people of God, gathered for a purpose and sent out to participate in its fulfilment. For most of us it will take some renewal, some re-evaluation of existing structures, to translate such a vision into practice.

If it is true, and we believe it is, that there is a great longing abroad to belong to something bigger and to be prodded and supported exactly where we are, how do we enter that company? How do we create and link up with such a vision? What mind-sets and what freedoms must we acquire? What will nourish us when the way is blurred and the going gets rough? That willingness and that search is the exploration into ecumenical spirituality.

In our own pilgrimage the first steps were those of dissatisfaction. The streams we came to drink from were dry, the air around us was heavy. During Gwen's nine years in Geneva she constantly sought for the centre, the heart, of the WCC. Where were staff nourished, centred? Where was vision rekindled? At times a living faith-community appeared, was tangible. However, there was a stark contrast in her visits to places of living faith and witness, such as St Benedict the Moor in downtown Milwaukee, where eucharist and the feeding of the poor went hand in hand.

The second step was Hanta Yo, to clear the way, to rid ourselves of the nonsense and clutter, the inner contradictions, the stifling dishonesties that stood in our way. Partly because of her own personal journey, partly because of her community's experiences, Joan had an ability to ask the awkward questions, to probe the externals, to lay bare the inauthentic and the unworthy. The story of "the emperor who had no clothes" was not lost on her!

Most of us carry a thick encrustation of half-baked theology, of guilt, of unreal expectations and split consciousness. The clergy have their baggage and the laity theirs. It weighs heavy, and inhibits life and growth and discipleship. We have imbibed and inherited distorted and inadequate spiritualities as well as authentic gifts of the Spirit. Some of us grew up on a religiosity that was separate from, and seemingly unaffected by, the needs of the world. Some of us bought into a consumer religion, pre-packaged and over-confident. Most of us practised a dualistic spirituality, separating earth and heaven, flesh and spirit. And often the result was a pietism that reinforced and strengthened the status quo.

It was our encounters with these expressions of a spirituality of withdrawal that prompted us to the explorations about which we write. We have come to believe that three essential ingredients of a revitalized and renewed faith are openness, connectedness, and earthedness.

How do we face reality as it is and be *open* to it? How do we let both the pain and the glory of the world flow through us? And then how do we discern our priorities, our individual and corporate responses to the divisions, the crises, the potential of our global village?

The reality of life is a tapestry, interwoven. Do we believe that our behaviour and life-style impinge upon and influence others, sometimes in far distant places? What does this belief in our *connectedness* mean to us as neighbours, church congregations, nations?

Our creeds and our philosophies must be incarnated in order to come alive and bear fruit. What are the local commitments through which we strive to create a more united, peaceful and just society? What are we *earthing*, wherever we are?

Even though we had originally started with reflections on the one, holy, catholic and apostolic church, we were driven, by the very life experiences people shared, to hew out these more human "markers". "The Christian life is not the creation of a separate kind of existence; nor is it the creation of a separate form of religious life; nor the following of an exclusively Christian way of life. Rather, the Christian life is the strengthening, promotion and celebration of all good and genuine human life."[12]

Pleading for a declericalized lay theology, Lesslie Newbigin writes: "We need much better provision to ensure that when church leaders make pronouncements on ethical, political and moral questions, their words are informed by a theology that has been wrought out at the coal face, at that place where faith wrestles at personal cost with the hard issues of public life. And we need to create possibilities in every congregation for lay people to share with one another the actual experience of their weekday work and to seek illumination from the gospel for their daily secular duty. Only then shall we begin to bring together what our culture has divided — the private and the public."[13]

Too many laity have "disappeared", been ignored, neglected, talked down to, until they have become passive or have passed out of the church doors in frustration. The visibility of the laity in some places is something like that of the handicapped husband in a wheelchair who was with his wife at a party. A well-meaning acquaintance joined them and offered to get them all coffee. "Does he take sugar?" this helpful friend queried. "Why don't you ask *him*?" replied the wife. Invisible and handicapped, handicapped by unnecessary burdens and atrophied gifts, many of today's laity await their cue. The Church of Scotland elder, the young artist from the US, the woman from India, have taken theirs. They belong to the ranks of those for whom the church is not defined by institutional structures or passive membership, but rather by the participation of God's people in the mission entrusted to them.

NOTES

[1] Lois Wilson, *On the Road to a New World*, Geneva, World Collaboration Committee, 1988, pp.14-15.

[2] John Tiller, *A Strategy for the Church's Ministry*, London, CIO Publishing, 1983.

[3] Ben and Carol Weir, *Hostage Bound, Hostage Free*, Philadelphia, Westminster, 1987, p.182.

[4] John Bell, "Tearing the Curtain in Two", *Coracle*, 1988.

[5] John Macquarrie, *Christian Unity and Christian Diversity*, London, SCM, 1975, p.25.

[6] Jurgen Moltman, *The Church in the Power of the Spirit*, London, SCM, 1977, p.10.

[7] Wesley Ariarajah, *The Bible and People of Other Faiths*, Geneva, WCC, 1985, p.70.

[8] Peter Fisker.

[9] Emmanuel Sullivan, *Baptized into Hope*, London, SPCK, 1980, p.142.

[10] Rosemary Haughton, *The Passionate God*, London, Darton, Longman & Todd, 1981, p.253.

[11] St Benedict's Mission Statement, Milwaukee, USA.

[12] J.A.T. Robinson, *The Difference in being a Christian Today*, London, Fontana, 1972, pp.17-18.

[13] Lesslie Newbigin, *Foolishness to the Greeks*, Geneva, WCC, 1986, p.143.

2. Openness

The open tomb is a symbol of resurrection. Mark records: "He is not here... He is going ahead of you into Galilee. You will see him there just as he told you" (16:6-7).

He is not here? He is in Galilee? But we thought we *knew* where Jesus was — in the life of our churches, in the words of scripture, in the blessed sacrament, in heaven at the right hand of God. What do you mean, he is not here, he is in Galilee? Not at the centre of power, not at the place of the religious establishment, but out at the ordinary crossroads of the workaday world, where people struggle to cultivate, and bring up families, and make ends meet.

"Why look for the living among the dead?" we read in Luke (24:5). What did the dazzlingly-clothed messengers mean? Are they suggesting we've been looking, well, not in the wrong places, but in not enough places? Some of our experiences of church are stale and nostalgic, it's true. And some of our gatherings, even ecumenically, are boring and dead-ended. Some of us haven't noticed recent trends in theology, or psychology for that matter, or attended any courses in contemporary spirituality or peace studies. Some of us pray the way we've always prayed, express our beliefs in the way we've always expressed them, practise our faith in the way we were instructed long ago.

You will see him there, you say? In the midst of the struggle and the pain of life? In the simple unnoticed signs of growth and renewal in nature? In the yearning and the efforts of human beings for wholeness and freedom? In everyday matters of economics and toil, of conflict and decision-making, in family celebrations and friendships?

> Life loom waits,
> and calls through myriads of faces
> in a collage of different tongues.
> How can we escape you?
> We cannot.[1]

The greatest of the Spirit's gifts, a friend has written, is that of openness, to God, to the world around us, to one another. Are we possessed by the same Spirit that possessed Jesus, "making him the most aware and sensitive and open human being who has ever lived... ceaselessly aware of God and fantastically aware of every person who crossed his path"?[2]

> Let in the fear,
> let in the pain,
> let in the nameless formless power
> that beats upon my door...
> How can a house so small
> contain a company so great?[3]

Are we attentive to the signs of the Spirit's renewing activity in our world?

> It's a long way off (the kingdom), but inside it
> there are quite different things going on:
> festivals at which the poor preside
> and the broken-hearted are healed
> ... industry for mending broken bones
> and minds fractured by life...[4]

In the past few years, sweating and searching with diverse groups, we have heard strangely-familiar and repeated stories of disappointments and disillusionments. We have listened to heart-rending experiences of frustrated ecumenical marriages, of blocks to intercommunion, of internal church-politicking. In so many places a narrow vision prevents us from seeing the largeness and rich diversity of life. More than thirty years ago J.H. Oldham wrote: "Christianity has no meaning for me whatsoever apart from the church, but I sometimes feel as though the church as it actually exists is the source of all my doubts and difficulties."[5] The swamp is a recurring image for us, ponds whose inadequate inflow and outflow leave them stagnant, thick with weed and decay. All of life, church life included, relies upon a creative inflow, fresh springs of growth and renewal, hope and energy. But it depends equally on appropriate channels of outflow, in interaction with and service to others, in generativity and generosity. Nourishment and vision are living water, but they overflow into engagement, witness and sacrifice.

Openness, constant and persevering, to influence and demand is something we naturally resist. Yes, it gives us access to the beauty of human relationships and the glory of our created world, but it reveals to us as well the world's pain and deceit and tragedy. Such exposure frightens us. We protest with Jeremiah: I do not know how to speak. I am only a child. We complain with Job: Why do the wicked survive, increase in age and in power? They do not feel the scourge of God. We are hesitant to accept the burdens of discipleship: I have called you friends, because I have disclosed to you everything that I heard from my Father.

Openness, to the demands, delights and disturbances of life, is a fundamental ingredient of Christian discipleship. The gospel summons us to awareness and compassion, to risk-taking and solidarity. If we are not fundamentally open, to see and to listen, to ponder, to question and to decide, to respond, the gospel will remain a story, an account, of another time and place, of other characters and their destiny. And this openness is not just for a few occasions, some hours of the day or week. Our vocation is to live as aware and compassionate Christians every day and for the whole of life. Every situation we meet requires some response.

One of our reactions is to protect ourselves. Understandably so. We can be so engulfed by need that we are unable to make any positive contribution. Some people suffer from a malady called compassion fatigue. They are torn between expressing and denying sympathy, between rushing out in concern and withdrawing in defeat and depression. We can become so overwhelmed by images of war and hunger, by tales of avarice and violence, that we are forced to tune it out, grow thicker skin, take flight behind our own barred doors.

Acknowledgment of our limitations is of utmost importance if we are to be committed for the long haul. Those limits are both personal and cultural. We have different gifts and different temperaments. And we all have our cultural blindnesses and prejudices. Tom Cullinan, a Benedictine, has written: "None of us is in a position to change the whole world, to change the entire structure of our society, but we are all able to do a certain limited amount. The danger is that we are not available to do the limited thing which is possible for us."[6] "To each of us divine grace is given... To some he gave to be apostles, to others prophets, or even evangelists or pastors or teachers. So he prepared those who belong to him for the ministry, to build up the body of Christ" (Eph. 4:7-13).

Our individual gifts and our real limits remind us that we must make choices. Those who wrote to us for this book shared some of their specific choices: I voted Green this year for the first time... I find my membership in the Fellowship of Reconciliation important... I tried out two simple experiments in my parish... I, a woman raised as a Roman Catholic, am now preparing for ordination in the Methodist tradition... I chose to live in an inter-cultural community... Our specific contribution is to open our home... I find my nourishment in the women's movement. We can all name moments when we opened a door, and thereby closed others, when we took the road less travelled by.

It is important not to confuse openness with keeping all our options open. Jesus steadfastly set his face to go to Jerusalem. He said to the Syro-Phoenician woman: It is not right to take the children's bread and cast it to the dogs. Jesus, open to all of life, nevertheless chose, decided — as must be. Crossing the road, crossing a border, crossing a threshold, but crossing over, says Robin Boyd, can be the moment of revelation and of conversion.[7]

Some of our choices may be life-changing, and not only for ourselves. Rosa Parks refused to move to the back of a bus and initiated a chain of far-reaching events. W.H. Vanstone's most profound book, *Love's Endeavour, Love's Expense*, was born after he put aside his academic appointments and gave himself unreservedly to parish duties on a housing estate. Beyers-Naudé moved from a position as leader in his own segregated church to leader of the anti-apartheid movement. "Truth normally only is revealed to us in situations of crisis, where you are forced into the crucible, where you have to make a choice... where it is no longer possible to say: I remain neutral."[8]

Wise choices presuppose discernment and discipline. Discernment is an art desperately needed in our crowded lives and complex world. And without discipline we will not stay with our choices once we have made them.

We Christians generally are not adept at discernment. Many of us are accustomed to being told what we are to do and what is expected of us. Some of us prefer behind-the-scenes politics to entrusting the outcome of a discussion or a proposal to the Spirit speaking within a community. Most of us want to exercise some control over what lies ahead. We are not too keen on waiting and listening, without prejudice, to each other, to our own inner instincts, to the quiet voice of the Spirit in unfolding events. We are often uncomfortable both with the element of desert that discernment requires and with the testing and trials that often accompany the Spirit's freeing truth. We still believe we can hold God captive within our human structures and rationales and we value human judgment more than the quiet, ambiguous messages we get from our prayer and meditation. Discernment, unlike so many of our human endeavours, cannot be scientific or foolproof. In that moment of truth, the important thing is to do the will of God, not to demand evidence or to manipulate the outcome.

> It will take some sawing, to be a round table,
> some redefining and redesigning.
> Changing a narrow-long church can be painful,
> for people and tables. [9]

Deeply and inextricably intertwined with openness is vulnerability. Many of us remain closed to our own brokenness. We seal off and disguise the wounds and blows life has given us. Yet, it is precisely where we have suffered and known pain that we can be instruments of life and hope to others. It takes courage to believe that, but we have all experienced it. Inevitably in our sessions, when Joan has shared a bit of her 1960s breakdown experience, with its tunnel of depression and its sudden severing of a budding career, questions and comments tumble forth about similar experiences. At a women's retreat in Canada, we found that it took only a few personal stories to open the floodgates of anguish and pain. Almost everyone in the room was ready to share her struggles of faith in the face of broken marriages, broken health, broken families, broken lives. There is a deep longing to redeem the scars and amputations. Offering them as a gift to others who walk the same path is a beginning. "Your pain is the breaking of the shell that encloses your understanding." [10]

We have often remarked that one of the reasons that St Ben's in Milwaukee is such an inspiring and credible community is because it is made up of people who know their own brokenness and can therefore hold one another in times of weakness.

Suburban parents whose confused teenagers have exhausted their willingness to forgive, the divorced man or woman, the alcoholic or chemically-dependent, the mentally handicapped, understand one another's brokenness. The unemployed man or the woman forced to accept welfare find their dignity respected and learn they have gifts nonetheless to exchange with other hurting human beings. "There is hope for a tree; if it be cut down, it will sprout again and its shoots will not cease though its roots grow old, yet at the scent of water, it will bud and put forth branches like a young plant" (Job 14:7-9).

We said earlier that our worlds (large and small) are both beloved and messed up and that therefore repentance and conversion are in order. It is openness that leads to conversion. When we begin to answer the question, what is really important, we are more likely to get rid of our baggage, our surplus props. Then fears and insecurities can come under scrutiny. And those prejudices and imperatives that keep us in bondage. In the story of the Good Samaritan, it was their moral imperatives that kept the priest and the Levite from responding compassionately to the man attacked by robbers. When our weakness is paramount, when we are forced to sort out our priorities, we gain a new perspective and are freed for what really matters. Those who have endured confinement together as hostages are not keen to make distinctions about whose worship they will follow or whose eucharist they celebrate. Those who are dealing with a life-threatening illness are prone to think anew about old patterns of acting and relating.

One crucial test of our openness is our ability to forgive. Is that not what forgiveness really means: keeping the door open for a renewed and more honest relationship? Jesus, says John V. Taylor, compelled Simon and Caiphas and Pilate to deal with someone who would not withdraw his offer of an honest human relationship.[11] Jesus reveals a God whose love places all at risk and whose vulnerability is extreme. There is no guarantee that the love offered will outlast and overcome the powers of hatred and evil. Openness to forgive is also openness to pain and rejection. Anne Lindbergh speaks on behalf of all mothers who have lost their children to violence and unnatural deaths:

> For whom the love locked up in the heart that is left alone?
> That golden yield split sod once, overflowed an August field,
> Threshed out in pain upon September's floor,
> Now hoarded high in barns, a sterile store.
> Break down the bolted door;
> Rip open, spread and pour the grain upon the barren ground
> Wherever crack in clod is found.
> There is no harvest for the heart alone;
> The seed of love must be eternally re-sown. [12]

A recent film on the first anniversary of the Armenian earthquake focused on a single family. The parents had survived but their children had perished. They were starving to be able to give love. Their real hope was the pending birth of another child.

A second test is the extent of our inclusiveness. One of the greatest temptations of religion is to suppose that it can contain God. We try to reduce God to something we can handle, enclose, ritualize, claim. It is this temptation, said J.H. Oldham, which leads the church "to compress the fullness of living reality into hard and fixed intellectual formulations and rigid moral codes and forms of activity which are too narrow to hold the rich exuberance of life". [13] We listen again to the prophet Zechariah: "There was a man with a measuring line in his hand. I asked him: 'Where are you going?' 'To measure Jerusalem, to find out her breadth and length.' 'Run and tell that young man,' the angel said, 'it is the Lord who speaks — I will be a wall of fire for her all round her, and I will be her glory in the midst of her!'" (2:5-8). No walls were necessary.

Speaking to the worldwide body of Anglican bishops at Lambeth in 1988, Elizabeth Templeton of the Church of Scotland challenged them with these words: "My first conviction is that there are no outsiders, all our outsiderness is to be regarded as provisional, since God's lively and inviting love is without bounds." "The church", she says, "exists to represent, cradle and anticipate the future of all our humanity... Any unity we seek must be to enact and articulate that... It must be the kind of unity which allows those outside to recognize their own humanness, to glimpse their own future with delight and hope, to get a whiff of their own transformation, their own wholeness." Are we ready to be converted to such openness? To be partners in discipleship, men and women, clergy and lay, Christians of all colours? And to undertake the profound changes such partnership will provoke?

Until 1981 Joan had never left the US. Even though she had been involved in justice and peace issues, she had not had an experience of other cultures, of the church in other lands. A three-month sojourn in India, in the hinterlands of Madhya Pradesh and Kerala, started her on a journey that increasingly taught her that *all* her worlds (US, RC, Franciscan) were too small. Gwen went to Africa as an ardent young disciple expecting to give her all. It was not long before she found it was Africa who was her teacher, that it was she who was in need of enlightenment.

Opening oneself to new challenges is an enlightening though exhausting process. Occasionally we do take a dramatic step that throws us into a completely new world. For most of us, however, there is a long series of hesitant responses, unbolting rusty locks, peeking through dusty windows, clearing a path through our accustomed furnishings. We found ourselves in the midst of a parable when we moved into Hanto Yo House. Before we could "open" it to visitors and guests, to the movement through it of pilgrims from many places, we had to clear it of the inevitable clutter of a quarter of a century. Drawers needed turning out, cupboards emptied of their dubious contents. We needed to create space in rooms overfull of furniture and cluttered with cushions and table coverings. Hallways needed to be lightened by fresh curtains and fewer obstacles. Not least, windows needed opening, in some cases, chiselling open, to allow fresh air and sunshine. Quite literally, we *opened* the house, much as our minds and hearts need opening so that the real world outside can enter and influence, or be encountered and grappled with.

At a specific stage in the disciples' ministry, Jesus questioned them. What are you telling the people about me when you are among them? Who are you saying that I am? No doubt Jesus meant more than the literal question contains. What does your witness say about me? What do people learn of me when they meet you? The question is relevant now: what is our witness, on this continent, at this moment in history, to the God in whom we believe? Does our discipleship reflect the generosity and the inclusivity of our God? Or is God minimized to suit the parameters of our secure, narrow system of beliefs?

When we dare to allow God to engulf us, we begin to reclaim the wholeness and the humanness of life. We refuse to split ourselves into compartments and categories, to split our consciousness into distorted and crippling patterns. We insist on a lived faith consistent with a God of justice and compassion. We refuse to "rank" vocations as if there were a divinely ordained hierarchy with all theologians and ordained ministers somewhere near the top and Christian lay women and men somewhere near the bottom. We try to be attentive to the Spirit, from whatever unexpected direction her winds blow.

If we have caught the spirit of an all-embracing God, we will begin to examine the standards by which we make plans and decisions, and implement them. We will build the values of community and respect for individuals into our work-related lives. We will take time to dwell apart, to commune in silence, to probe deeply and constantly the connections between our local affairs and our global home, our faith and our life.

Finally, we will be about the tasks of freeing ourselves and one another from our bondages: to law, to unrelenting traditions, to society's complicities with injustice and oppression, to the narrow visions of those who would imprison the God of life. We will painstakingly risk the unmasking of our arrogance, the divesting of our dishonesty, the exposing of our manipulative minds. We will, bit by bit, arena by arena, die to those attitudes that seal us off from the refreshing abundance and the simple gratuity of God's gifts. Then the swamp will become the river of life. Or to change the image:

> Rountabling means:
> being *with*,
> *a part of*,
> *together*, and *one*.
> It means room for the Spirit,
> and for gifts,
> and for disturbing profound peace for all
>
> ... Wishing and hoping
> will not get us there —
> daily dying and rising will
> (and some sawing).[14]

NOTES

[1] Chuck Lathrop, "Life Loom", *A Gentle Presence*, Washington, DC, Appalachian Documentation, 1977, p.25.

[2] J.V. Taylor, *The Go-Between God*, London, SCM, 1972, p.17.

[3] Kathleen Raine.

[4] R.S. Thomas, *Later Poems, 1972-82*, London, Macmillan, 1983, p.35. We are keenly aware of the problems the word "kingdom" creates. In some cases we have chosen to retain it, to be faithful to the context. At other times we have replaced it with a phrase that seemed appropriate.

[5] J.H. Oldham, *Life is Commitment*, London, SCM, 1953, p.79.

[6] Thomas Cullinan, quoted in *Peacemaking: Day by Day*, Pax Christi, USA, p.127.

[7] Robin Boyd, *Ireland*, Geneva, WCC, 1988, p.103.

[8] C.F. Beyers-Naudé & Dorothee Sölle, *Hope for Faith*, Geneva, WCC, 1986, pp.26-7.

[9] Chuck Lathrop, "In Search of a Round Table", *A Gentle Presence, op. cit.*, p.5.

[10] Kahlil Gibran, *The Prophet*, London, Heinemann, 1926, p.61.

[11] Unpublished paper on forgiveness.

[12] Anne Morrow Lindbergh, *Hour of Gold, Hour of Lead*, New York, Harcourt Brace Jovanovich, 1973, p.183.

[13] J.H. Oldham, *op. cit.*, p.88.

[14] Chuck Lathrop, "In Search of a Round Table", *op. cit.*

3. Connectedness

A decade ago to speak of our interconnected world or the tapestry of life was still a novelty. The events and discoveries of recent years have forced upon us the knowledge that all creation coinheres, that the web of life in which all is connected is a reality. Chernobyl, the death of the Amazon forest and the destruction of the ozone layer are common coinage of the 80s. An array of witnesses bears testimony:

> The deeper reality is our oneness in God, one earth, one life, one nature. To understand this is to understand the basic message of authentic religion but it is also to understand (stand in) the basic truth of the universe. It is to stand in the deepest truth of existence — that we are all part of one life on one planet that is itself part of one cosmic creational event. What happens to the earth and to the "other" happens to ourselves... Scientists are exploring the smallest particles of matter and the far reaches of space and beginning to discover empirically what spiritual visionaries have known intuitively. The universe is one. All is inter-related and bound together. [1]

> One creature sustains another, one enriches the other and that is why all creatures are interdependent. (Meister Eckhart)

> No despair of ours can alter the reality of things, or stain the joy of the cosmic dance which is always there. Indeed, we are in the midst of it, and it is in the midst of us, for it beats in our very blood, whether we want it to or not. [2]

> This we know. The earth does not belong to man (sic); man belongs to the earth. This we know. All things are connected like the blood which unites one family. All things are connected. (Chief Seattle, 1854)

> God sits weeping.
> The beautiful creation tapestry
> She wove with such joy
> is mutilated, torn into shreds
> reduced to rags
> its beauty fragmented by force. (M. Rienstra)

> Glance at the sun. See the moon and the stars. Gaze at the beauty of earth's greenings. Now, think. What delight God gives to us with all these things... All nature is at our disposal. We are to work with it. For without it we cannot survive. (Hildegard of Bingen)

> The universe as such is the primary religious reality, the primary sacred community, the primary revelation of the divine, the pri-

mary subject of incarnation, the primary unit of redemption, the primary referent in any discussion of reality or of value. For the first time we can tell the universe story, the earth story, the human story, the religion story, the Christian story, and the church story as a single comprehensive narrative.[3]

For Christians, or people of the Book, it is salutary that it has been scientists and people of primal cultures who have retaught the world that central mystery of our interdependence for good or for ill. It is there deeply in our faith, in the Bible, and in the writings of many mystics. But as Thomas Berry says: "Nature gradually disappeared from Christian consciousness."[4] The heresies of individualism, of personal salvation at the expense of other concerns, the divorce of sacred and secular, have led us on false paths. The prime minister of the UK, a practising Christian, is able to forcefully declare: "There is no such thing as society, there are individual men and women and there are families." In keeping with this belief, her governmental policies have unleashed greed and competition, and contempt for those who cannot or will not join in the scramble for self-betterment.

Much of Christianity is still captive to that kind of thinking and practice, but happily in the process of shaking itself free and rediscovering its own heritage. It is ironic that the old enemy science should be one of the most significant resources for a bigger and deeper faith. Writing in the *Guardian* newspaper, Keith Hudson says: "Fings ain't wot they used to be in the world of science. The hard, logical certainties of reality are giving way to an almost magical world that lies underneath... Everything appears to be connected together in a most intricate, yet funda-mental way. In the words of Sir Fred Hoyle, 'Once the universe is seen as an intrinsically linked loop, nothing can be discarded. Everything exists at the courtesy of everything else.'... There is now an agonizing plea for a unified belief system, new metaphors, a universal set of values, a common agreement about the significance of life and — nearer home — acceptance of the stewardship of the planet."[5]

All things are connected. The belief of the mystics and the poets. The controversial insight of Charles Williams, spelled out in both theology and fiction. Out of that long tradition, Rosemary Haughton writes: "Life in this context means all of reality, all that is and could be, and it involves thinking of everything not just as part of an infinitely complex web of interdependence but as a moving web, a pattern of flowing, a never-ceasing in-flow and out-flow of being... (of love actually), a constant flow of energy which is actually the experienced nature of relationship of all kinds."[6]

Feminists are today insisting on this reappraisal of reality. There is a popular poster produced by the Women's Sub-unit of the WCC in Geneva quoting the phrase: "I am — because I participate." The background of that statement is not well-known. In the 1950s the International Missionary Council began a series of studies on the life and growth of the younger churches. John V. Taylor went to Uganda and immersed himself in village life. That experience led him to describe the central understanding of the people as not "I think — therefore I am", but as "I participate — therefore I am". The statement resonated with many Africans and was quoted by Rose Obianga at the Community of Women and Men in the Church world meeting. It has frequently been used since to express women's understanding of the way life is.

If interconnectedness is the way reality is, then it should be no surprise that we keep stumbling across it, as we dig deeper into our own Christian tradition. This is the strength of so many liberation theologies, be they minjung, Latin American, black or feminist. They challenge mainstream Christian thought and life as they ask fresh questions, heal the splits that have developed. These splits are pervasive, affecting some of our basic assumptions, leading us down narrow paths of partiality and exclusiveness. So much of traditional Christianity is concerned with relating to a God who dwells in some inaccessible spiritual realm. Yet, another thread of our tradition does speak of God as covenanted to and present in people. God is revealed in living experience. Sexuality, for example, is an expression of our spirituality. Salvation is not only personal and individual, but a social process that transpires in community.

Perhaps most of us who have been brought up in the alienated West stumble over this when we fall in love. The world is then illuminated; we *know* all things belong and coinhere. But the hard work of day-to-day relationships, of persevering discipleship, is to live out that vision. Jesus lived in the reality of the oneness of life, a life where all interpenetrates and thought and deed affect and spread good and bad infection. "O marvellous exchange! Our Creator took flesh. We have been made sharers in the life of God, who was humble enough to share our humanity." It is a story of exchange. The secret of discipleship, of spirituality, is the uncovering of this life of exchange and the commitment to live this reality, in the way of Jesus. It is a way of reciprocity, of mutuality, of vulnerability, of hospitality.

In Philippians St Paul describes the process of emptying and receiving, of influencing and renewing, that Jesus underwent in the incarnation. "Have one love, one spirit, one feeling, do nothing through rivalry or vain conceit. On the contrary let each of you gently consider the others as more important than yourselves. Do not seek your own interest, but rather that of others. Let what was seen in Christ Jesus be seen in you: though being divine in nature, he did not claim equality with God, but emptied himself, taking on the nature of a servant, made in human likeness, and in his appearance found as human. He humbled himself by being obedient to death, death on the cross" (2:2-8). It is the same process and vocation to which we are called as disciples and which we are to incarnate within our own history and culture. As we root ourselves in and are enriched by the authentic values of our culture, as we live and express the gospel in ways meaningful to us, our very witness will confront and challenge aspects of that culture. No one space or time can claim to be Christianity's vessel. It is in the fullness of the human family that we see the many faces of Christ. The gospel is good news to every culture and never just comforting news.

This insertion and mutual interaction describe the life of families and neighbourhoods, congregations and nations. No one in any of these units is self-sufficient, nor is any unit self-sufficient. No one can fulfill the mission alone. Families thrive when each member has a role, a recognized place in the whole. Neighbourhoods are sustained and grow when there is a healthy exchange, an atmosphere of mutual effort for a common good. Congregations and communities come alive when clergy and laity, women and men, old and young, are partners in ministry. Internationally we are instruments of one another's well-being or destruction.

How many times have we said that the privilege of the ecumenical movement is its opportunities for dialogue, for reciprocal encouragement and correction, for an exchange of gifts! Events all around us are putting flesh on that vision. Not only church members, but people of all persuasions are demonstrating the value and the necessity of bridging our divisions, joining the common tasks that confront human community. The formal ecumenical movement can take lessons from recent developments, in Eastern Europe, in the growth of the Green Party, in the multi-mannered expressions of concern and commitment to the world's children.

One of the places that has experienced a convergence of energies and dreams is Brazil. A recent report spells out this transition from new perception to renewed discipleship and a new way of being church.[7] A movement comprising some 80,000 little communities has sprung up from the people. The existence of these base communities teaches a new mode of belonging, of participating. They bridge the divides of clergy and laity, prayer and politics, Sunday and weekday, women and men, church and world, Bible and life. It is people on the edges, the poor, women, third-world Christians, who are leading us to a deeper understanding of the one church for the one world. It is they who will broaden our horizons for hope, nourish our weak efforts to uphold the innocent and comfort the anguished, and provide leadership in the struggle with opposing systems and structures. Perhaps they will prompt us to explore the meaning and direction of base communities in our own regional context, that is, new ways of being church. "If the world is experiencing a new exploration into the meaning of human community, the church must explore the meaning of Christian community anew. If there is a radical attempt to return to the roots of being human, there must be a radical attempt to return to the roots of being Christian. Such exploration and radical attempts are described as 'base communities'."[8]

Unfortunately, we are more likely in our everyday life to be conscious of the areas where connectedness has been broken in our churches and in society. We have all discussed the greenhouse effect and the dangers of pesticides, the Rushdie affair, the polarization over women priests. We have all been scandalized by overt racism, sexual harassment, the laws that prosecute homosexuals. We are not all keen to name these "refusals of exchange" as sin. But generically that is what they are. They include oppression, exploitation, greed, self-righteousness, indifference, and prejudice. Isaiah puts them in their proper framework: "If you remove from your midst the yoke, the threats and the wicked word, if you share your food with the hungry, and give relief to the oppressed, then your light will rise in the dark, your night will be like noon. Yahweh will guide you always and give you relief in desert places. He will strengthen your bones, will make you as a watered garden... Your ancient ruins will be rebuilt, the age-old foundations will be raised" (58:9b-12).

The gospels echo the contradictions of separation and hostility in lives that are meant to be interdependent and related. "Yahweh has put down the mighty from their thrones and lifted up those who are downtrodden" (Luke 1:52). "Fortunate are you who are poor, the kingdom of God is yours... But unhappy are you who have wealth, for you have been comforted now" (Luke 6:24). "Come, you blessed... I was hungry and you fed me... Go away, you cursed... I was a stranger and you did not welcome me into your house" (Matt. 25:34ff.).

The whole of human life is the locus of discipleship. Our parish boundaries, our arena of concern, our outreach, is to extend to the whole earth, to those near and those far. "Now you are no longer strangers or guests, but fellow citizens of the holy people; you are of the household of God" (Eph. 2:19). Our movement towards unity is one with the renewal of the human community. Racism is a denial and a sin against the unity of the body of Christ, as it is a block to harmony and justice within society. "There is no question", writes Leonardo Boff, "of prayer on one side, and action on the other, nor of a prayer separated from practical commitment to the liberation of the oppressed. Rather there must be prayer in the process of liberation itself and an encounter with God must be experienced *in* the encounter with our brothers and sisters."[9] We may debate whether the appropriate response to Christ's prayer that all be one is unity in prayer, theological unity, unity in mission. We may debate which are the confessional issues and which are social issues. The truth is, prayer means commitment, and freedom and human dignity and reverence for creation *are* theological issues. Gutierrez speaks of the complementariness of the prophet and the contemplative. "Without the prophetic dimension the language of contemplation is in danger of having no grip on the history in which God acts and in which we meet God. Without the mystical dimension the language of prophecy can narrow its vision and weaken its perception of the God who makes all things new. Each undergoes a distortion that isolates it and renders it inauthentic."[10]

At one conference/retreat centre in southern England "spirituality" events are over-subscribed while the offer of comparable events on the theme of justice have had to be cancelled due to lack of interest. Melvyn Matthews comments: "What I think is true is that many people who go on retreat do not allow the experience of retreat... to transform their whole lives and release compassion and action... It is also true that those who are involved in the struggle for social justice treat their struggle as simply a matter of political action. The actions are not tempered and shaped by an awareness of love and compassion... My concern is to bring these two sides of the coin together and not to force them apart."[11]

Conversion to this awarenesss of our interconnectedness will transform and inspire the spirituality we live, personally and in common. The eucharist becomes *the* rite of exchange. "There is no greater love than to lay down one's life... This is my body, given to you." The eucharist is the place where we glimpse what happens when the life of Christ encounters the structures of this world's order. We will recover the connection between the washing of the feet and the sharing of bread and wine. The eucharist is constructive of community or it is not eucharist. We will recover the relationship of the needs of the world, the hungry, the forgotten, the captives, to our commitment to become bread and solace and friend for one another. "Unless the bread and wine come off the table of our common lives, then it is not our real lives we are asking God to deal with."[12] Furthermore, there will be no line around the eucharist. The exchange will be a continuum from bread broken daily to celebrations among Christians facing possible death. All will be doing this "in memory of me". And when we do, some of our denominational differences will seem like mere squabbles in the face of the transforming task to which we are called and for which we need both sustenance and empowerment. "As the eucharist has become the place where our separation is most obvious, it must become the place where our witness to unity in the Spirit is most powerful."[13] It is summed up in *Baptism, Eucharist and Ministry:*

> The eucharist embraces all aspects of life. It is a representative act of thanksgiving and offering on behalf of the whole world. The eucharistic celebration demands reconciliation and sharing among all those regarded as brothers and sisters in the one family of God and is a constant challenge in the search for appropriate relationships in social, economic and political life... The eucharist involves the believer in the central event of the world's history. As participants in the eucharist, therefore, we prove inconsistent if we are not actively participating in this ongoing restoration of the world's situation and the human condition.[14]

Intercessory prayer will become a means of growth in awareness and growth in unity. The daily news, the Ecumenical Prayer Cycle, our personal contacts, will be woven into one movement of concern and advocacy. Our prayer will inspire us to act and our action will force us more deeply into prayer. "When you stretch out your hands, I will close my eyes; the more you pray, the more I refuse to listen... Put an end to your wickedness and learn to do good. Seek justice, give hope to the oppressed; give the fatherless their rights and defend the widow" (Isa. 1:15). If we persevere in prayer in this framework, other changes will follow. We will read the scriptures with new eyes and against the backdrop of our own times. Congregational prayers will be more inclusive. Our sermons and religious education courses will take up the theological and moral implications of today's burning issues. Gradually our own petty resentments, our private weapons, our violent habits, will be revealed to us.

Personally and ecclesiastically, our life-styles will come under judgment. Others *are* where they are, in conditions of poverty, misery, despair, because we are comfortable, secure, and upwardly mobile. We will take responsibility for our educational opportunities and the privilege of our private homes or rooms, the luxury of times of solitude and of recreation. More of us will take leadership in critiquing our social and economic systems and in supporting the prophetic voices within our community and church circles.

The depth and scale of human suffering will impel us to reflect on what it means to talk about God, justice and the communion of saints. Our consciences will be challenged, and silence before oppression, at home and afar, will turn to protest. "I will not restrain my words, in the agony of my spirit I will speak out and complain with embittered soul" (Job 7:11). Our own sufferings, which include job and money worries, marital and family struggles, the dreariness and monotony of difficult commitments, pressures of time, will lead us to a more radical communion with all who anguish. Like our prayer, we will make our wounds and our scars available to others.

We will expect our families and our Christian circles to be inserted into this pattern of shared struggle and shared resources. To be identifiable as places of refuge, of hospitality, and of conversion. Our commitments will be more informed and we will seek to make our ministries, our value systems, more consistent with the gospel's priorities. We will be more conscious of the detachment and the gentle, non-violent spirit of the man from Galilee, and refrain from empire-building, ruthless competition. We will be more generous and more forgiving.

The new rapprochement in Europe between East and West, as well as the significance of 1992 for Western Europe, presents an enormous challenge to that continent, a potentially wealthy super-power, to acknowledge its connections to poorer parts of the world and to share its resources. Will it be an overfed, fortressed Europe, or a welcoming, hospitable and generous community?

As our discipleship is renewed, we will welcome and maximize our status as laity, as the people of God, who make up the church. When necessary we will resist being cast into the position of "those who listen and those who pay". Our baptism ushered us into a community of equals. As such, we bless, we teach, we ordain one another. We will not be discouraged from articulating our faith, our response to God's word, our belief about any issue that touches our personal and communal life. We will work together for a catechesis that is meaningful to youth and for a liturgy that is the expression of the whole people of God. Our liturgies will arise from life: its bereavements, its seasonal wonders, its passages and breakthroughs. As business people, as families, as educators, as students, as media creators and participants, we are the carriers of Christianity.

These are the implications for our discipleship. They are costly. We will experience displacement, misunderstanding, conflict, and perhaps exile. Prisons have become sacred places in many parts of the world. Some Christians have deserted their careers once they have recognized the contradictions between the work of their hands and the word in their hearts.

Each of us must discern what solidarity with our brothers and sisters means in our circumstances and how we will express it. How we will stand with villagers and farmers in Asia and Africa, with prisoners of conscience, with abused children, with the unemployed, the lonely and alienated. We begin where we are.

Once we acknowledge the truth of our membership one of another, not only with our heads, but with our resources and our choices, we will demand of ourselves a faithful stewardship. Not limited to tithings or annual collections, but inclusive of our health, our talents, our possessions, and our use of earth's gifts. One proposal suggests that one way of helping third-world debt would be for countries who have sold arms to these countries to buy them back at full value! We all owe a portion of the debt of these countries. Famine in our world should affect us all. The children of the world belong to all of us. We begin where we are.

And finally, we will make reconciliation, in our personal lives, among our churches, and in society, our mission. "All this is the work of God who in Christ reconciled us and who entrusted to us the ministry of reconciliation" (2 Cor. 5:18). A first step towards reconciliation is healing. And human beings cannot heal without grieving. Therefore, we must recall our history together, endeavouring to stand in each other's places, endeavouring to understand one another's languages and sacred stories. We also cannot heal without facing the hard truth of our common humanity and our potential for sin, misjudgment, competition and arrogance. Forgiveness, it has been said, is both a sign of humility and of acceptance. We are all offspring of Adam and Eve. Only when we ourselves are willing to disarm and surrender will the fires of violence and hatred abate. In the end, reconciliation entails dying: to our grievances, our self-certainties, our individualism.

In the film story of Gandhi there is an unforgettable scene between Gandhi, ill from fasting, and a despairing Hindu. "I'm going to hell," said the Hindu. "Why?" whispered Gandhi. "Because I killed a child. I killed a child because they (the Muslims) killed my son." "I can show you a way out of hell," Gandhi said. "Go find a boy, a Muslim boy the age of your own son. Take him in, raise him as your own. But", Gandhi looked straight into the man's eyes, "be sure you raise him as a Muslim."

It is that generosity of spirit, that openness to the flow of healing and new life that marks the followers of the one who washed his friends' feet at his own farewell meal, who recognized the plea for acceptance in every human being, who, when he was lifted up on the cross, drew all things to himself in a loving embrace.

NOTES

[1] Patricia Mische, "Toward a Global Spirituality", *Whole Earth Papers*, No. 16, p.10.
[2] Thomas Merton, *New Seeds of Contemplation*, London, Burns & Oates, 1961, p.230.
[3] Anne Lonergan and Caroline Richards eds, *Thomas Berry and the New Cosmology*, Mystic, CT, Twenty-Third Publications, 1987, p.37.
[4] *Ibid.*, p.16.
[5] *Guardian* newspaper, 9 March 1987.
[6] Rosemary Haughton, *The Passionate God*, London, Darton, Longman & Todd, 1981, pp.21,23.
[7] "Renewal from the Roots", report of WCC team visit to Brazil, May-June 1988.
[8] Emmanuel Sullivan, *Baptized into Hope*, London, SPCK, 1980, pp.196-7.
[9] Leonardo Boff, *Mysticism and Political Action*, quoted in *Doing Theology in Different Contexts*, a Latin American-Central/Eastern European dialogue, 1988, p.30.
[10] Gustavo Gutierrez, *On Job: God-Talk and the Suffering of the Innocent*, New York, Orbis, 1987, p.96.
[11] *The Tablet*, 23 September 1989, p.1092.
[12] J.A.T. Robinson, *On Being the Church in the World*, London, Pelican, 1969.
[13] Anne Primavesi & Jennifer Henderson, *Our God has no Favourites: a Liberation Theology of the Eucharist*, London, Burns & Oates, 1989, p.66.
[14] *Baptism, Eucharist and Ministry*, Geneva, WCC, 1982, E.20.

4. Earthedness

Nothing is real which is not earthed. Incarnation is concrete. It happened at a particular time and in a particular place. Disciples are European or Malaysian or Australian or... They are men and women, locally rooted, in dialogue with all the specific realities that surround them: their environment, their schools and churches, their cultural events, markets and farms, their network of friends and relatives. In this context, our philosophies and creeds take flesh. For most of us, the fruit we bear is stamped with a local print, on offer to our neighbours and members of our immediate circles.

We understand ourselves to be an intentional community which draws great strength from the eucharistic presence of Christ and from our prayer and worship with one another. In a spirit of love and care, we welcome all who worship or gather at St Ben's. Tolerance in our community fosters pluralism in our faith. We are enriched by the diversity of talents and giftedness in each individual. We support and affirm one another in our varied ministries (from St Ben's mission statement).

Members of the Iona Community share a fivefold rule, which commits its members to daily prayer and Bible study, stewardship of time and money, corporate life and accountability, and prayer and action for justice and peace at every level (from the Rule of the Iona Community).

The whole community of Holly Springs has an international flavour. We are Northerners, Southerners, blacks, whites, Indians, Pakistanis, Nigerians, Kenyans... Living here reminds me that each person's story, journey, is at some levels everyone's story. Each individual nation is every nation (letter from a friend).

How can we live the gospel as middle-class white Australians is a question that we often ask ourselves (letter from a friend).

The world is big, but it is also the little space under my feet and within my reach. Is it too much to ask each person to love the creation, travel lightly, share your sandwiches, pick up your own garbage, be ready to lend a hand, and make friends? (comment from a student)

We aim to create at Hanta Yo House a living cell which will nurture an ecumenical spirituality... Our focus will be on how we live as disciples in our world today, that is, not in denominational bondage, and intimately involved in the realities of contemporary life... (initial proposal of Hanta Yo House).

> He began thrusting his iron rod into the earth, making a hole in which he planted an acorn; then he refilled the hole. He was planting oak trees (from *The Man who Planted Trees*).

Jesus spent the first thirty years of his life in one place. He earthed himself in the soil of Nazareth, then Judea and Galilee. He was a carpenter, a layman. He went faithfully to the synagogue where he learned the scriptures and listened to the rabbis. When he began his public ministry, he wandered from village to village accepting hospitality and building a small community of disciples. He chose twelve. He experienced frustration with the legalisms of church officials, felt the pressures and fatigue of too much human interaction, knew the pain of bereavement and rejection and false accusation. He honoured the simple human beings whose lives brushed his: the fishermen, the young wedding couple, the lame and the blind, the woman accused of adultery. And he lifted up the simple signs of faith and of life: a newly sown field, a little child, a storm at sea, bread and fish. He did not classify people into artificial groupings. Everyone, friend or foe, merited his honest word and the challenge of his ubiquitous paradoxes. He obeyed law, but he was also able to set law aside. He understood the immediate needs of those who came to him, but he managed to draw them beyond themselves into new territories and new questions. Jesus was a sign of openness and connectedness, of the local and the global, of contemplative and prophet, of human being-ness.

And so it is to be with those who follow. The word is to be made flesh again and again and dwell among us. We are to be concrete embodiments of the gospel mandates. Some seem to have succeeded in capturing the spirit and the vision: Francis of Assisi, Hildegard of Bingen, William Temple, Mother Ann of the Shakers. Others nearer to us have inspired and led us: Dorothy Day, Oscar Romero, Florence Allshorn, John XXIII, Janani Luwum. Most of us are at best ambiguous signs, with high hopes and good intentions, failing and falling, rising again, prone to all the hesitations and vagaries of the would-be disciple. Who do you say that I am? Of what are you a sign? What do your words and your life point to? What is the lasting fruit for which you and you alone are accountable? And what do our Christian communities and churches say about the one whom they profess to follow? How easily recognisable are they as signs of hospitality, of forgiveness, of compassion, of sacrifice and commitment? What does the World Council of Churches incarnate, in Geneva, in its commissions and conferences, in the life-style of its staff? What kind of sign are our local councils, our ecumenical bodies and agencies?

We believe that the ecumenical movement and its purposes are bigger than interchurch relationships. The ecumenical vision and challenge constantly push us out of our church-iness to a more global, more kingdom-oriented obedience. This is its cutting edge. If our councils, local, regional or world, are places where Christians meet, worship, debate, act jointly, on issues of church and society, then they are exciting foretastes of that which is not yet. Then they are something worth belonging to. They must model in their own life what is expected of individual Christians, a global vision and a local concern. Too often our larger ecumenical bodies are shockingly affluent, run along business models, self-perpetuating and in-turned, rather than generating and nourishing communities of discourse and a confessing church. It would be salutary to analyze the participants of the WCC's global meetings since Vancouver to see whether the same old boys' club turns up again and again and whether many genuinely new laypeople are brought into them. Is the WCC spawning, from its exciting and expensive world gatherings, groups of people with vision for the local, ready to immerse themselves in that local? Or is it simply creating a taste for international church jet-setting?

In stark contrast to global gatherings are those isolated places where some go out and down to work at one task under lonely circumstances. One story we have often used is *The Man Who Planted Trees* by Jean Giono.[1] He tells the tale of Elzéard Bouffier who turned a "barren and colourless desert" in the Alps into a fertile land by planting trees. For thirty-seven years Bouffier planted, first acorns, then lindens, beeches, birch and maples. Streams long dry began to flow and willows grew again. Villagers and hope returned. It is a modern parable of the mustard seed, a parable of the new creation. Elzéard Bouffier found the one thing he could do. "It was his opinion that the land was dying for want of trees."

It is hard for some of us to believe we can actually make a difference, in the face of the complexity and size of the systems that engulf us: political, economic, technological. One of our correspondents wrote: "Let us shine in our local small places. Let us give taste to the small quantity of food which is so important to our local community. Let us pray that the ecumenical movement will spread like a wildfire close to the ground and not like well-prepared fireworks which illuminate the sky and give pleasure to the spectators just for a little while only." Let us believe in the acre we are planting and tending. Another wrote: "I am part of a local Christian fellowship. It has no formal structure. We meet in our homes. We share reflections and experiences of our pilgrimage over coffee. We care for each other." It was H.A. Williams who said: "The place where we feel most at home, the people we most deeply love, the works of genius which have fired our imagination, these are instances of the Word being made flesh and dwelling among us, and thus creating us."[2] In Dorothy Day's words: "By crying out unceasingly for the rights of the workers, of the poor, of the destitute, we can, to a certain extent, change the world; we can work for the oasis, the little cell of joy and peace in a harried world. We can throw our pebble in the pond and be confident that its ever-widening circle will reach around the world. We can give away an onion... We can enlarge our hearts to love each other."[3]

Some years ago a group of religious women in the US gathered for a weekend in Washington, DC. They recognized the need to be involved in the legislative process as intelligent citizens and as lobbyists. Bills pending in Congress: a national health service, reform of the criminal justice system, foreign military aid, affected the lives of those among whom they ministered. Out of that initial brain-storming of the handful of women was born a national lobby, Network. In the next ten years it had local branches in each of the fifty states and expanded from a membership of exclusively religious women to other committed laity.

In 1964 Jean Vanier, the son of the governor general of Canada, made a personal choice. He welcomed two mentally and physically handicapped men into his home. This gave rise to the movement called L'Arche which now exists in twenty countries through eighty-five small communities.

Many years ago Henry Thoreau wrote: "I know this well, that if 1,000, if 100, if 10 honest people — ay, if 1 honest person in this state of Massachusetts, ceasing to hold slaves, were actually to withdraw from this co-partnership and be locked up therefore, it would be the abolition of slavery in America. For it matters not how small the beginning may seem to be, what is once well done is done forever. But we love better to talk about it... There are 999 patrons of virtue to every virtuous person."[4]

We do not always know the ripples our lives make. Surely the persistent vigil of the women on Greenham Common and at other military sites had its effects on the winding down of the nuclear missile bases, whether or not any political entity ever admits it. Surely our friend who has taught secondary students for thirty years has had a lasting influence on a generation of youth. Surely the eighty-two year old woman who has washed dishes nightly at the meal programme at St Ben's since it began has been a sign of magnificent generosity.

In the early days of Christianity, individual households provided the hospitality, the platform, and the economic security for fledgling preachers and teachers. At the heart of daily life, in small communities, Christianity was nurtured. These domestic churches realized the fundamental value of a community which shares its faith in a concrete way within the social context of its times. Often women were the leaders in these households: Phoebe, Prisca, Lydia, Tabitha. Theory and praxis went hand in hand. Is it not time to restore the concept of "households of faith", of neighbourhood? Have not St James, Piccadilly, the Corrymeela Community, Taize, Imshausen, made a difference to the marginalized, the hurting, the youthful searchers? We at Hanta Yo House are learning the mutual benefits of opening our house to visitors and offering a bit of space and a welcoming peaceful atmosphere, of working and playing and praying in the one locus.

Who was neighbour to the one who was beset? Jesus asked. Are our lives places where faith, comfort, healing, hope, are being discovered? Could Christians be integrating factors in neighbourhoods uncertain of their future, grappling with economic forces or racial struggles? Certainly Christians can be interrogating factors in the society: what is the church *for* in this locality? Why are there unemployed when so many needs are unmet? What are the priorities of this government? Will we allow our environment to poison our children? Our slow and persistent efforts can resow fields neglected or overgrown. We can provide some steady penetration of the ordinary milieus in which we live with an extraordinary concern, for human needs, for justice for all.

Base communities, such as those that have grown so widely in Latin America, base communities adapted to the particular culture in which they form, are a sign of the future. They are the "tip" of a phenomenon that goes deeply into the people's movement that is swelling in different parts of the world. Rosemary Haughton says: "These small 'basic communities' of mostly lay Christians are visibly the place where the reborn church is growing... This is the new body of Christ, growing from within the old situation, reaching out and recreating in Wisdom's way. Men and women work together as equals in a way characteristic of the new church everywhere."[5] "The most dynamic, Catholic feminist movement in the 1980s", says US theologian Mary Hunt, "has not been ordination but women-church. By 1983 when change was not imminent, many Catholic women formed base communities. We stopped knocking on the church's doors and begging admittance. We began simply to *be* church."[6]

The point is that we must all find the circle, the community, that receives our gifts, shares our values and vision, and supports us in our efforts to realize them. It may be a local congregation, it may be an already existing framework within the Christian community, but not necessarily. There are a plethora of small groups, networks, fellowships, shooting up all around the world, meeting the needs of the time, adapting to the exigencies of life in the world, endeavouring to be part of the new creation.

Whether we act alone or within a group, we need staying power. Not only do we need to continue to pray together and to communally discern. We need also to hang in with issues of local environmental concern, local services, local farm issues, until right decisions are made. There can be no retreat from our commitments. "I think that staying power is a quality we need very badly and that very few people have. They seem to lack long-term courage, that creative patience — not the sort of patience that is basically a sort of apathy, but the sort of patience that knows how to go on and on until the end appears — to hang on to the vision until it is possible to be creative with it, and not to give up one's vision just because things seem to be hopeless... That staying power calls on deep spiritual resources, on a deep peace within ourselves."[7]

Some of our most admired friends in the ecumenical movement have been at it for years on end: Hans-Ruedi Weber, Lesslie Newbigin, Pauline Webb, Aled Davies, Andrew Hake, Jean Skuse, Ted Scott, Lucille Evans, Max Thurian, John Yoder... We need to become like those who refuse to accept second-hand solutions and who struggle their way to an authentic life-style, an authentic expression of gospel values. It is a long road to freedom, as the song tells us. And as the Nelson Mandelas, the Lech Walesas, Hung Kyu Parks, Marga Buhrigs, know. It took us eight years of journeying to find the base from which we could launch some of our long-held dreams.

Perhaps an essential ingredient of discipleship today is "dwelling among", being inserted into, our specific communities, histories. Jesus "dwelt among us". Authentic gospel ministers have always been those who dug in deeply, who took on the particulars of a culture and a people. That is difficult for executives of big agencies. That is difficult for church people who remain within their enclosures of office and church property. To be "all there" is to be genuinely local.

A famous sculptor once said: "Before I ever touched metal, I used to go out and sit on a rock and look at nature. Sometimes I spent hours looking at bugs crawling along on the ground... One day as I looked at those leaves and bugs and trees, I began to see the forms of nature. I began to see beyond and through the tiny things to the vast and sweeping forms of eternity. And then I began to sculpt."[8] A reason, no doubt, why we often give up, or fiddle endlessly with trivial changes, is our difficulty in seeing. We aren't willing to stand, or stay, long enough to recognize the deeper need, the unique contours, the life-giving direction. It is perhaps the most abiding and significant gift of the currently maligned missionary era of the late nineteenth and early twentieth centuries, the Gladys Aylwards and Trevor Huddlestons and Frances Cabrinis, who buried themselves in one culture.

That so few saw the need within their *own* culture is of course the judgment on that enterprise.

As we enter more deeply into our experiences of disillusionment, we may at last grasp the message underlying it. We may need to let go of our romantic images of community and of church, and find new ways of gathering that nurture and illuminate our true vocation. "Since this is a vision for an appointed time, it will not fail, but will be fulfilled in due time. If it delays, wait for it, for it will come" (Hab. 2:3). Perhaps what we can do is clear the way, dwell among, develop staying power.

Whatever shape and style our commitments and communities take, they will nonetheless need ongoing renewal, clearing of the way, if they are to be fruitful. A Syrian Orthodox bishop, now in the US, comments: "I am now 58 years old and still do not know the significance of beards in the history of salvation!"[9] We so often get locked into external forms and confuse real change with the essential heart of our faith, and our conduct with certain visible rituals or symbols. The rearranging of church furniture or ecclesiastical dress is not enough. The more significant question is: what is our mission and are we prepared for it? Another Eastern Orthodox theologian asks: "Is our liturgical life meaningful enough to be shared with newcomers? Or is it functionary only in terms of providing comfort and satisfaction to our present membership?" And then the final query: "Is it possible that the life-giving Spirit, which is always vivifying the church, made her freeze at one point in history?"[10]

The Spirit speaks afresh in each generation. The Spirit had different messages to the churches of Pergamum, of Ephesus, of Smyrna and Sardis. What is the Spirit saying to the church in Britain, in this era of privatization of industry, of deepening divides between north and south, of increased homelessness? "We have seen with our own eyes our society being driven in a direction that contradicts the gospel... As we survey our society, our inescapable conclusion is that many are being hurt in Britain today, damaged and discounted by public policy."[11] What is the Spirit saying to the church of Europe in this historical movement of freedom and self-determination, with the opportunities for greater exchange and mutual reliance? Or to the church in Africa as a recent report makes clear the downward spiral of this continent?

In Annecy in 1985 a small sampling of disciples from different parts of the world and from different churches met to search together for the direction in which the church is being led in this time. It identified some of the marks of an ecumenical spirituality. It is lived and sought in community. It is nourished by prayer. It is expressed in service and witness. It is ready for risks, willing to become a confessing body. It is open to the wider oikoumene. [12] Annecy described an "earthed" people with a task to detect where and how God is acting in our world and to make their lives available to those purposes.

Too often we are busy "keeping things going", maintaining our plants, holding our family and business lives together, surviving ourselves or ensuring the survival of our pet institutions. We have not time nor inclination to listen, to discern, to question, to probe. The call to renewal means that we take time to diagnose the state of our spiritual journey (personal and communal), that we identify gifts for ministry, our own and others, that we encourage the development of a theology of work, of stewardship, that we experiment with methods of prayer, meditation, decision-making, leadership. The spiritual life is a pilgrimage, not a cyclic routine. Work is needed on opening our liturgies and our sacraments to actual human experiences, on reclaiming the unity of life and faith, on challenging social structures in church and society.

If our church gatherings are not structured for mission, we must recreate them. If new ideas are forthcoming, in worship, in styles of ministry, in extending outreach, in deepening our understanding of our roots and our charism, we must encourage and undergird them. If questions are raised by minorities in our midst — lesbians, single or divorced men and women, youth, people of other faiths — we must engage those groups in a free and honest dialogue. Integral to renewal is the death of old structures and patterns of living. Some of our institutions and even some cherished parts of our traditions may have to die or recede. But in the letting go and in the new spaces created, a clearer vision of what is needed may be born. Why is it that it is so often the marginalized who ask the probing questions? They do not have investments in the status quo. They experience the sting of oppression. And it is from those channels that the call for radical change often springs.

Finally, we must take the risk of breaking new ground. Perhaps this moment calls for signs, small signs of new life, of brave witness, of magnificent generosity. Over and over we hear similar reactions to the "high" moments of a Basel conference or a Vancouver assembly or a Moscow meeting. The Vancouver tent was a sign of pilgrimage and openness. The walk through five countries, the tightrope across the Rhine, the Jericho roses, the stone of witness, were signs of the integration of faith and life. The Moscow meeting with its opportunities to see and participate in the life of Russian churches was a sign of religious as well as political perestroika. The first thing Gwen did when we moved into Hanta Yo House was to clear a space and plant a *sign* in an untidy garden. Overwhelmed by the magnitude of the gardening task, she created a tiny bed of beauty and welcome. Small ecumenical communities, Local Ecumenical Projects, base communities, women-church, are signs that new ways of being church do exist.

People's theology is no longer a fringe effort or the crusade of a small minority. Some people in congregations today are lifting their heads and their voices. Bent over like the woman in the gospel for so many years, women and men are straightening themselves up to a full life worthy of their humanity and their priesthood.[13] The cries of the minjung, the courage of the Brazilian slum-dwellers, the vision of contemporary prophets, lead the way. A new church *is* being born.

We may inch along in the matter of recognizing one another's priesthood and ministries, but in many ways interdenominationalism is a past issue. One of our seasoned friends commented recently: "The ecumenical movement is wasting its time on healing denominational rifts. The Holy Spirit is way out ahead in the small groups which are already post-institutional church, living, witnessing, celebrating a new reality."

As far as the eucharist is concerned, "waiting" for intercommunion is no longer an acceptable solution. Nor are "multiple" eucharists the answer. We had an unforgettable lesson in the sheer ridiculousness of such in Switzerland at a small ecumenical gathering. In one brief weekend we attended three eucharists (Roman Catholic, Orthodox and Reformed). At no one of them did/could the entire group communicate. We do not believe that "enduring the pain" of our separation is what God intends in those circumstances. Rather, it may be a modest equivalent of "self-flagellation". If there is a spiritual reality and actual unity experienced and named, it is to be celebrated. "Let us negotiate for unity at the top," Robinson wisely said, "but let us press forward through intercommunion from below. Let the one loaf be the spiritual reality that compels us to greater unity."[14] "The eucharist shows us that our behaviour is inconsistent in face of the reconciling presence of God in human history: we are placed under continual judgment by the persistence of unjust relationships of all kinds in our society, the manifold divisions on account of human pride, material interest and power politics and, above all, the obstinacy of unjustifiable confessional oppositions within the Body of Christ."[15]

Interchurch marriages are already a thorn in the flesh of some church officials. But perhaps they must become even thornier. Apartheid under any name is sinful. How can a situation be justified in which one spouse's religious, aye Christian, beliefs are secondary to the other's, in which full religious union is made impossible, in which children are deprived of the benefits of an ecumenical formation from the beginning of their lives, in which the bodily union of marriage is negated by the community of faith which exists to celebrate it?

In the real order of things, there are no certainties, no guarantees of complete rightness with no margin for error. We search and struggle, we make mistakes, we muddle through, we ask the wrong questions and we take incomplete answers as the full truth. We learn, by trial and error, how to discern when to act and when to wait. We confuse the urgent and the immediate, patience and passivity. But such humanness was never an obstacle to Jesus' gift of himself or of his approval. The only grievance Jesus had was with those who *claimed* to see and to know, those who put unnecessary burdens on others, those whose own lives were a contradiction, and those who refused to allow human frailty and human differences. "Do not prevent the children from coming to me" (Matt. 19:14). "Not even in Israel have I found such great faith!" (Luke 7:9). "Simon, I have a bone to pick with you..." (Luke 7:40). "Those who do not see shall see, and those who see shall become blind" (John 9:39).

42

NOTES

[1] London, Peter Owen, 1989.

[2] H.A. Williams, *True Resurrection*, London, Mitchell Beazley, 1972, p.96.

[3] Quoted in *Peacemaking: Day by Day*, Pax Christi, USA, p.143.

[4] Source unknown.

[5] Rosemary Haughton, *The Passionate God*, London, Darton, Longman & Todd, 1981, p.275.

[6] Quoted in *Chrysalis: Women and Religion*, November 1989, p.3.

[7] Thomas Cullinan, quoted in *Peacemaking: Day by Day, op. cit*, p.135.

[8] From a paper by Michael Allen, "Teaching Students to see the Patterns of Eternity and Hope".

[9] Philip Saliba, "On Being Orthodox in America", *Ecumenical Press Service*, 21-30 September 1989.

[10] *Ibid*.

[11] Declaration by Church Action on Poverty, Manchester, UK, December 1989.

[12] *A Spirituality for our Times*, Annecy report, Geneva, WCC, 1985.

[13] Sermon by Marga Buhrig, WCC Central Committee, Moscow, 1989.

[14] J.A.T. Robinson, *On Being the Church in the World*, London, Pelican, 1969.

[15] *Baptism, Eucharist and Ministry*, Geneva, WCC, 1982, E.20.

5. Blocks, Captivities, Splits

"This people pays me lip service, but their heart is far from me; their worship of me is in vain, for they teach as doctrines human commandments. You neglect the commandments of God in order to maintain human traditions" (Mark 7:7-8).

> Religion indeed enslaves people... When a denomination becomes a power in itself, concentrating on its own heritage of doctrine, order, or worship rather than on "the solid reality which is Christ's", the denomination, or this particular confession, has become a semi-divine power and needs to be dethroned... All religious activities, teachings and ministries that are man-made (sic), and that allow Christians to be anything more or less than people who share God's mission to the world, are enemies of God, and Christ will ultimately bring them under his feet. [1]

> If we insist that God can only act and bless when certain conditions are fulfilled, we show that we believe in God in a box. Some of the old Hebrews thought they had the covenant because they had God in a box. They needed to learn that the true God of covenant is free as air, always going ahead of them in shining cloud and fire. The box became so unimportant that it is not even recorded when they actually lost it. But the pillar of cloud and fire still marches on. [2]

> What will happen to narrow-long ministers,
> when they confront a round-table people,
> after years of working up the table
> (as in "up the ladder")
> only to discover that the table has turned round? [3]

When we took on Hanta Yo House in mid-1989 we acquired a large garden. Most of the garden was neglected and overgrown. In one area, hidden among the riotous weeds, was a rose garden. There was barely a bloom to be seen, much dead wood and old roots. After a preliminary weeding to see what was there, we embarked on a ruthless pruning of the dessicated branches and twigs, then a feed of phostrogen for nutriment and copious watering in the rare drought we were experiencing in Britain. There was some limited response. Clearly more drastic measures were needed. On hands and knees we excavated the earth around each root until it lay bare to a depth of a foot. There, clearly visible, were choking stifling white creepers of the virulent couch grass common in this region, tough tendrils wrapped tightly around the rose roots and absorbing all available resources. The work of patient removal of every bit of this strangling growth was wearying and time-consuming, but a *sine qua non*. We had no idea what, if anything, would bloom. As the days and weeks passed, it was deeply rewarding to see buds form, unfold and reveal to us their own unique being: floribunda, hybrids, scarlet, yellow, orange, white and pink. Now as we write, some months later, the bushes are vigorous, healthy and blooming. Clearing the way is our job. The growth and flowering follow.

We are convinced this is the pattern for renewal today. Clear the way, so that life may flow, nourishment be received, growth happen and fruit appear. Jesus' fiercest denunciations were against those who blocked the way for others. "You prepare unbearable burdens and load them on the people..." (Luke 11:46). "You have taken the key of knowledge. You yourselves have not entered and you prevented others from entering" (Luke 11:52). "You devour the property of widows while making a show of long prayers" (Luke 20:27). "You do not forget the mint, anise and cummin seeds when you pay tithes, but then you do not fulfill what is most important in the law: justice, mercy and faith... You strain the mosquito, but swallow a camel" (Matt. 23:23-24).

We want to name some of the obstacles which need to be removed in order to set ourselves free, as God's people, for growth and fruitfulness. There is a huge variety of life in many of our churches. Some are vigorous and vibrant. We speak in what follows of those places where a fullness of life does not flow and where the fruit promised by the Spirit is absent.

Maintenance and membership, or mission: our club churches

In much of Western Christianity today, the life of faith is almost exclusively centred on the church building and its Sunday worship. The largely all-male clergy, whether priest, minister or pastor, "run" the church club for its membership, that is, those who attend, those who pay their dues and for whom the once-weekly nourishment is prepared.

In the city of Guelph in Canada, comprising around 80,000 people, there were forty-three churches of a variety of denominations. All were financially viable and all offered a variety of diets to the faithful. This one has "lovely music", this one was "evangelical", this one catered for "yuppies", this one was pre-Vatican II, and so on. We were struck by the similarity to a shopping mall, where shop-keepers side by side decorated their windows and lured consumers inside to buy their wares and thus keep them (the shopkeepers) in business. Church relations in Guelph were good, partly because the forty-three churches were still sustainable, that is, enough money came in to keep the plants and the pastor going. But the movement was "in". With a few notable exceptions, the churches acted precisely as clubs, drawing members and money for the perpetuation of their own life and interests. Those who run the clubs need to please their clientele. And indeed, with such a variety of choices, it is easy to switch churches, much as one switches channels on television.

This description is by no means limited to Guelph. Attendance at Sunday services in countless places will illustrate the emphasis that exists on maintaining property, sustaining clergy and staff, offering a menu of social and liturgical events to the membership. Where mission is a concern of these club churches, it is interpreted as efforts to increase the membership. The spirit in these congregations may be friendly and welcoming, but it is more or less confined to an inner circle. There seems to be little recognition of the world beyond the club church's boundaries, little readiness to respond to the drastic demands of the gospel to reach out and to reach out further and further. "The real evil of working competitively, self-interestedly, exclusively, parochially as Christians needs to be exposed and experienced, seared into our faith. Our failure to face the world, and hide instead in the church... our contentment with patterns of privilege, power and territory that stunt and deform spiritual growth, with models of ministry that foster dependency... can only be confronted with each other's courage."[4]

Passivity and participation

It should not be possible, but is, that a Christian visiting a church for worship speaks to no one from the time of entry to setting off for home again. The understanding of once-weekly corporate worship as an intensely private conversation between God and the soul is still around. In some Anglican churches in

Britain, the congregation *refuses* the kiss of peace because "it disturbs the flow of the liturgy".

"I go to church to be fed," say many older people. While the young people say: "I don't go to church because I'm fed up." During Gwen's time of working locally in East Anglia, she had many discussions with a local vicar about renewal. Her stress on participation was heard and some occasional efforts were made to find a reader other than the vicar. Between the reluctance of those asked and the priest's heavy burden of five services each Sunday in rural villages the effort died an early death. Far easier to do what everyone seemed to accept, that is, treat those attending as a pudding over which one poured an appropriate sauce, as well-cooked and flavoured as possible. The collusive grumbling about "our clergyman" and his ways, or "my lay people" and their ways, are all symptoms of the sickness of a church which is not a church, a church whose life has ceased to flow even though it has deep and ancient roots in Christian faith and tradition.

An extremely able and creative lay woman theologian was recently asked a year in advance to take over a congregation of Presbyterians for a three-month stint while the minister was on leave of absence. She agreed. Some nine months beforehand she was met with a demand for advance notice of her preaching topics. "How can I possible know beforehand what will be pertinent?" she responded. "I don't know what will be happening in the world at that time." The demand was insistent. "Very well," she said, "next Sunday allow me a few minutes at the end of the service." Armed with paper and pencils she requested the congregation to suggest a topic they would like her to preach about during her three-month ministry. Enthusiastically, the people contributed their ideas, to the open-mouthed amazement of their regular minister. No doubt, he had never before witnessed such a consultation of consumer concern!

One begins to understand the movement of church women, the needs identified by base communities, the opting out of so many intelligent and sincere seekers, when one sits Sunday after Sunday in a church where sexist language is rampant and sadly not even an issue, where connections are rarely made between contemporary events and the day's gospel, where the divide is abundantly clear between those who are ordained and those who are merely baptized. So many conversations we have endured with clergy who joke, who preside, who condescendingly question, but who, in all honesty, do not take women or laity seriously. Or perhaps they do, and dwell behind the defensive postures they have so carefully developed: jest, graciousness, aloofness.

Some of this clergy-laity problem is reinforced by the concentration in theological colleges and seminaries on the academic side of training. While much has been done to improve theological education, to broaden and deepen it, it is still a common experience for mature and seasoned lay Christians to be subject to the wordy ramblings of a raw young man straight from college in the name of a "professional" priesthood.

Discipline or discipleship

The issue which focuses most sharply the discipline/discipleship question is intercommunion. Here is a real denominational/confessional bondage, whether we're trapped *in* an exclusive eucharist, or excluded *from* one. It feels deeply wrong to most lay people. The more shared experiences there are, the more people press forward against the barriers put there by *men*. Do any of us dare to say we are excluded by *God*? That *Jesus* forbids us to come to his table? We know we are invited and we do not believe that accepting that invitation depends on our capacity to do mental gymnastics in relation to the elements. Come all who believe in the Lord Jesus Christ. Come all who try to serve him. Come all members of his body, weak in faith, but needing the food of the faithful. Our discipleship demands an open table, yet we are refused this by the discipline of many churches.

When we began to work as a team leading retreats in the search for an ecumenical spirituality, we had one particularly stark experience of the muddle and confusion in our churches over eucharistic sharing. We were a group of twenty, together for four days, meditating together on the meaning of the one, holy, catholic, and apostolic church. As a very mixed group, we had planned to end with an agape or para-liturgy. The RC priest, an ecumenical officer, who was attending decided to hold a pre-breakfast mass. We were all welcome to attend, but only the RCs could receive. (There were 7 RCs in the group, 5 of them sisters.) This announcement followed immediately upon a presentation on the inclusive church where there was neither Jew nor Greek, slave nor free, male nor female! No one was excluded! The contradiction was stark. It was evening and we had already agreed on silence until breakfast! We as leaders were in a particular dilemma and others were busy trying to sort out their own response and feelings. In the end people went every which way! Some stayed away, including two RC sisters, some went, one RC sister fasted with the Protestants to show solidarity, one Anglican man felt honoured to be given a blessing, etc.

There was no way the retreat could continue without some airing of the situation. After breakfast we had a lengthy and frank sharing. Every one of the twenty people present spoke. The sharing itself was a clear breakthrough. There were some tears. For some it was the first time they had been publicly open with their feelings and thoughts about the matter. The Spirit was at work in our brokenness and we did go deeper as a result. But it is too facile to say that we should keep church discipline in order to feel the pain of separation. Our own practice in groups now is that we will not have a separated eucharist. We prefer to have a simple agape in which all share and where we experience unity and communion. With regard to our own practice as a team outside groups we have decided we will not be separated. Either we both receive, or we refrain.

We have entered into countless discussions and debates on the "whys" and "why-nots" of intercommunion. Repeatedly we have heard the fears of clergy, their own insecurity, the theological arguments, doctrinally based, the warnings put to us as mere laity who are "embarking on a path the dangers of which we couldn't possibly grasp". What has happened to the primacy of individual conscience? Why has the eucharist (God's own gift) been locked up in doctrinal safekeeping? Why is the interpretation of Jesus' own words, "Do this in memory of me", reserved to an elite few? In the words of a friend: "Because God accepts us unconditionally, so must we too receive one another. We cannot talk about our unity if we do not visibly express it." Has not the time come when we must choose between discipline and discipleship? Is the eucharist that time and place?

Splits, one-dimensional faith

Perhaps one of the greatest of our captivities today is our dualism. We live as split people. Faith is one-dimensional, it belongs to the private sphere, it addresses itself to personal morality. We have lost the sense of all life illuminated by the gospel and the whole of our interaction with others as challenged by the gospel. "Respectable" Christianity is shocked by involvement in politics. In Uganda the revival fellowship expelled anyone who became a politician. In Washington, DC, a leading evangelical speaks of the prayer meetings of evangelical Congressmen where not one prayer relates to US foreign or domestic policy. The prayers are for "my daughter Susan on drugs" or "our marriage under stress" or "my suicidally-depressed grandson". Thanks be to God Congressmen pray and pray for others, but what is the Good News to all creation if it is locked out of those public spheres where human agony is equally felt? Policies are faulted and countries sin as well as individual human beings.

A sermon extolling the work of those who smuggle Bibles into Russia has been seen as consonant with the gospel. But using the Sanctuary Movement as an illustration in a sermon is regarded as subversive.[5] A member of parliament recently attacked church leaders for meddling in politics (as they dared to speak out for the poor of Britain). The same MP holds a place in the Synod of the Church of England!

The locking up of faith in a box is one of the most paralyzing blocks to vital faith today. Individuals live split lives where private morality and public morality exist in opposition, where spirituality and sexuality wage a neurotic struggle, where prayer is a running away from life instead of an entry into deeper life.

These splits lead directly to the narrowing of an understanding of mission. Mission becomes a converting of others to my way of thinking, or my special experience of Jesus or the Holy Spirit. The vast sweep of God's mission is lost, because the fullness of faith and gospel, "to the ends of the world", is lost. "The true perspective of our lives is not the small, moderate bourgeois world that we pretend is ours but a cosmic stage on which the great extremes of the gospel are stark realities — light and darkness, life and death, luxury and starvation, heaven and perdition."[6]

Writing many years ago, Father Kelly, founder of the Society of the Sacred Mission said:

> To us theology was not a technical and professional knowledge. We were studying God's view of human life — what God was doing on the Somme, and at Westminster, and at Tilbury Docks.... I do not want to know what you can do with Christ in a church (building) half so much as I want to know what Christ is doing in the street... The worship of the parish church is the key which should unlock the mystery of God in the world... This is the age of the laity, and the witness of the church is primarily in their hands.[7]

Static bureaucracy versus dynamic movement

> It is said that when the British Council of Churches was set up in 1942 Joe Oldham suggested to William Temple that the ecumenical movement had been set back a generation. We can certainly see what he was getting at. To give institutional form to a movement not only marks the start of a new era by trying to embody the mood and needs of the time, it also represents a hardening of the arteries and a formalizing and narrowing of vision. There are both gains and losses and the losses may be as important as the gains.[8]

Renewal movements are breakthroughs. New life flows from the energies released. Sometimes begun by an individual with a special charism or by groups gaining new vision, their evolution is such that within decades many have become institutionalized. That which flowed, was supple, found its way around obstacles, or broke through them, is now itself ossified, hardened. The history of the church is full of such examples. Within the Roman church the flow is literally *order*-ed and thereby a balance is achieved of reception of the new insights and control of the energy. Within Protestant churches there is a tragic history of splitting off, excommunicating, and of exaggerated claims in relation to *a* dogma. The Orthodox insist on renewal *of* the old and reject the breaking through of the radically new.

The origins of the ecumenical movement lay in springs of insight and obedience in many places. These came together in three broad streams: Life and Work, Faith and Order, and the International Missionary Movement. The student movements fed, nourished and interacted with these. In 1948 the second world war was over, the USA was wealthy and *in* Europe. And a heretofore embryonic WCC was birthed as an organization.

Over the years a complex bureaucracy grew up, designed to safeguard the various communities of discourse and their interests.

Sadly, it seems that all current ecumenical agencies have adopted an "office model". Alec Vidler, in his autobiography, tells of an old invitation to head up the British Council of Churches. In his reply he wrote:

> If what we want are secretaries who will take over the London office… and begin by carrying on the whole show as it is at present though with the possibility of much subsequent transformation, then I must say not only that I do not feel called to it, but that I feel called not to do it. On the other hand, which seems very unlikely, if the BCC were contemplating a fresh set-up which no doubt would have to include a London office and some of the machinery which is at present centred there, but which has as the centre of its life and activities a sort of ecumenical centre in the country… where there would be a group of people living and thinking, praying and worshipping, together — where both groups and individuals could come and stay — from which it was hoped that the ecumenical understanding and spirit would grow and radiate, perhaps leading to the setting up of similar centres elsewhere in the country — well then, if this were being seriously contemplated, I should feel very differently about any call that was made on me… But I fear it is so improbable that a transformation would be effected at the outset that it is not worth my saying any more about it…[9]

In a recent survey of the ecumenical situation in East Anglia, Gwen found local (town) councils of churches dying under the weight of a business style — agendas, minutes, chairpersons, and much boredom. Sparsely attended and supported only by ecumenical enthusiasts. How utterly different the experience of mixed groups gathered to search and to share their common pilgrimage, knowing themselves as church, called to be together in mission!

Many agencies today are searching for ways to make their offices places which "live" what they *do* and *proclaim*. "The church must cease to be looked on primarily as an institution and be treated as a way of being. The church is primarily *communion*."[10]

All the above are examples of the clutter, the couch grass, the captivities, which need to be cleared away and destroyed that we might live, and be leaven and light and salt. They relate to two false understandings: First, what and who is church? And second, what is the calling of the church? It is only as we all deeply understand the truth that the whole people of God are the church that we will find release from the domination of the clergy, the passivity of the laity, or be able to receive the gifts of women and young people or others who are excluded. We still do not know *we* are church. It is the great liberating truth, affirmed by Vatican II, discovered by base communities or small gatherings of committed people ready to share search and pilgrimage. Comprehending the church as the whole people of God ensures that relationships are seen in personal terms, rather than hierarchical. It ensures the place of history in the dynamics and processes that develop. In ensures that the boundaries are flexible, merging into the whole human race. [11]

> In families and groups of families, in small temporary groups of college students, in groups gathered for social action, in groups gathered for prayer, in residential communities and in neighbourhood ones, in professional groups, groups in prison, in church halls or living rooms, on college campuses or in motherhouses, in all these ways and places, people are coming together, trying to find a way to make sense of their lives, to *be* the future by letting it grow out of the depths of themselves. [12]

Perhaps the waning numbers of clergy and the loss of buildings in many places may be a blessing forcing people to rediscover the essentials of being church. Small communities have helped to put the Bible and its interpretation into the hands of people. It is no longer the prerogative of the priest or the theologian. Its interpretation is no longer limited to theological categories but includes everyday life experiences. Base communities suggest that community centres, where prayer, worship, politics, and practical courses can be integrated, are more necessary than churches reserved exclusively for religious services. One church in Halifax in northern England has become a parish that functions out of an old vicarage. They no longer worry about hassock repairs, an antiquated boiler, or a leaky bell-tower. Instead their new quarters house meetings, classes, a family centre (for Muslims too), and a small modern chapel. "The freedom from the burden of a church building has made the people understand what a church really is, a presence and a gathering place among the people of God."[13] Not a building, not the priest, not a Sunday special diet, but clusters of people together seeking to be open to the Holy Spirit and then to be obedient to our calling.

And what is this calling? Not the cultivation of my soul, not even the good works I do, but the willingness to say *yes* to God's purposes, to incarnate the small bit of the whole which it is given to me to flesh out. To be open, connected, and earthed, and, like those rose bushes, freed of strangulation to bear fruit as a part of the whole. "I am the vine and you are the branches. The one who dwells in me bears much fruit. Apart from me you can do nothing... This is my Father's glory, that you bear fruit in plenty and so be my disciples... You did not choose me; I chose you. I appointed you to go out and bear fruit, fruit that will last" (John 15:5,8,16).

NOTES

[1] Albert Van den Heuvel, *These Rebellious Powers*, London, Billing & Sons, 1966, pp.71-2.

[2] J.V. Taylor, *Winchester Churchman*, 1982.

[3] Chuck Lathrop, "In Search of a Round Table", *A Gentle Presence*, Washington, DC, Appalachian Documentation, 1977.

[4] John Bluck, *Everyday Ecumenism*, Geneva, WCC, 1987, pp.68-9.

[5] John Bell, "Tearing the Curtain in Two".

[6] J.V. Taylor, *Weep Not For Me*, Geneva, WCC, 1986, p.4.

[7] Quoted in Margaret Dewey, "Thinking Mission", USPG Publication, January 1987, pp.6,8.

[8] Paul Ballard, *The Modern Churchman*, Vol. 30, No. 4, 1989.

[9] Alec Vidler, *Scenes from a Clerical Life*, London, Collins, 1977, pp.132-3.

[10] "The Forgotten Trinity", British Council of Churches, 1989, p.29.

[11] John Macquarrie, *Christian Unity and Christian Diversity*, London, SCM, 1975, p.42.

[12] Rosemary Haughton, "There is Hope for a Tree", unpublished paper, 1981, p.7.

[13] *Guardian* newspaper article.

6. Vision and Resources for Vision

In *The Prophetic Imagination*, Walter Brueggemann speaks of the threat that imagination presents to many people. "Our culture", he says, "is competent to implement almost anything and to imagine almost nothing."[1] Certainly the church is influenced by our culture. And many of us experience it as adept at implementation and deprived of creativity. When it comes to structuring or restructuring, to organizing a course or a stewardship drive, to formulating policy or proposals for synod, the church and its myriad institutions are often expert resources. Many of us would concur that our church bodies are far less visionary when it comes to prophetic ministry or to styles of leadership and interaction that inspire and liberate.

Recently we attended an ecumenical prayer service for peace in one of our local churches. It had been well advertised and we expected to join a sizeable community. About a dozen gathered. We recognized early on that the "leader", the local curate, had brought no imagination to the event: last-minute preparations, a complete lack of participation, falling back pathetically on the service books in the pews. Whether or not he was embarrassed by the slipshod results, he could comfort himself with having fulfilled his duty to "take the service". The poster, which we had admired, had been more imaginative than the service itself.

Often in our ecumenical comings and goings, we have noted and been appalled by the lack of vision. Imagination seems to extend as far as exchanging pulpits, hosting common events, occasional joint Bible study, and the appointment of an ecumenical officer (usually a clergyman). The Lund dictum notwithstanding,[2] actually planning together, maximizing personnel, joint financing, and structuring departments in an ecumenical mode, are foreign to many bodies and officials. "New spectacles are needed which 'see' the total church situation... a genuine conscientization which at every turn asks the ecumenical questions. On every agenda the first question should be 'Is this a priority?' and the second, 'How can we do this together?'"[3]

Is not the actual situation in many of our churches, where women are frustrated, laity are discouraged if not absenting themselves, youth are proclaiming themselves agnostics, that of the people perishing from lack of vision? One young man in Limerick, Ireland, told us that if he did rejoin a church (he was raised as an RC), he would choose a Protestant church because he perceived that Protestants at least asked questions. His view of his own church was one of passivity, docile obedience, and utter irrelevance. Another young man whom we know, product of an excellent education and with a degree in engineering, had a vivid conversion experience and wanted to go into full-time lay ministry. He gave up his career to do so, but is currently at an impasse. The openings available to him are so limited and lacklustre.

Often in our reflections or times of prayer, that particular New Testament passage has leapt out at us: "See the fields white and ready for harvesting" (John 4:35). In John's gospel, those words follow upon Jesus' proclamation that his real food was doing God's will and carrying out God's purposes. It is in relation to mission that Jesus described "the sheep without a shepherd". "Jesus went around all the towns and villages, teaching in their synagogues and announcing the good news of the realm of God and curing every sickness and disease. When he saw the crowds he was moved with pity" (Matt. 9:35-38). And in Luke's gospel, the reference to the abundant harvest is in direct conjunction with his sending of the seventy-two disciples into mission (10:1-3).

A further look at the commissioning reveals the "vision" that Jesus had in mind for both disciples and those to whom they were sent.

Firstly, *the growth of the realm of God is immediate and urgent*. "Tell these people: God's realm has drawn near you" (Luke 10:9). *God is at work in our world*. That work may be *hidden*, in the healing hands of refugee workers, in the gentle words of primary school teachers, in the silent prayers of forgotten people, in the generous self-giving of parents and community workers. But it exists, and it quietly extends its redeeming, reconciling, renewing effects. The new creation grows like a seed, spreads like yeast, seasons like salt. That work, the building of the new creation, may be *visible*, as the light cast by a lamp, visible in its attractiveness and its warmth. It may be visible as the cross is visible, in the combined suffering of those who resist injustice and announce peace. The realm of God is among us wherever God's action is recognized and proclaimed, wherever people live out, amid struggle and doubt, amid the daily exigencies of economics and societal pressures, indeed amid the contradictions of religious institutions, some portion of the good news.

Secondly, *the approach of the disciple is to be clear and simple*. "I send you out like sheep among wolves... Set off without purse or bag or sandals... where you are not welcome, shake the dust from your feet" (Matt. 10:7-16). *The mission we undertake is God's mission*. We are all inadequate messengers, all fragile vessels of God's weighty word. We are to resist cluttering our discipleship with unnecessary baggage: our own petty agendas, our ego-trips, our tendencies to build small "kingdoms" of our own, our yearning for publicity and acclaim. We are not to waste time or talent on deaf ears and closed minds, but to offer our gifts, meagre as they may be, to the open-handed, the poor, those who hunger and thirst for a new breath of life.

Thirdly, *there is an intimate, unbreakable connection between the disciple and the one who sends*. "Whoever listens to you, listens to me... You will be brought to trial because of me... A student is not above his or her master" (Matt. 18:24; Luke 10:16). *We walk in the footsteps of the cross-bearer, the foot-washer, the friend of the broken and the outcast*. We will bring down on ourselves the rejection Jesus knew, we will find community in the homes and hearts of those who are meek, who mourn, who are themselves merciful. We will share the loneliness, the passion, the prayer, the sacrifice, of the Human One.

If that is the vision with which Jesus commissioned his disciples, if that is the life they were to embark on, what does it mean for us in this century, in our present world? Everything we have written points to the necessity in our age of being the one church for the one world. The realm of God is near, everywhere on this globe. When Christians from South Africa count on Christians in Europe and America to join them in their journey of liberation, the realm of God is near. When Witnesses for Peace from the USA take their places at the side of Nicaraguans on the borders with Honduras, the realm of God is near. We share the new freedoms of the Eastern Europeans, the efforts for reconciliation of the Sri Lankans, of the Christians of Northern Ireland. In our attentiveness, in our spiritual bonds, in our movements of solidarity, we seek to be as global as any secular institution, as committed to the merger of the divided segments of our family as any multinational corporation.

We must be clear and simple about what we affirm, what we choose. And we must shake off the dust of fear and complicity. Where there are new sparks of life — circles of women-seekers, experiments with community, alternative institutions of healing, gatherings across divisions of whatever nature — let us encourage. Where there are power-plays, political games, competitive wrestling, stagnant and nostalgic versions of liturgy and education, let us leave that milieu. Let us affirm those who take the risk of opening their tables, those who risk critique and sanction for their pioneer work in theology and spirituality, those who facilitate the exchange of gifts and insights. The frontiers of God's realm cannot wait for approval under every circumstance, for official endorsement. Loyalty to tradition does not preclude imagination, honest dialogue and critique, or brave exploration. Some will find their vocation in struggling within the institutions to restructure and to renew. Others will find it at the fringes, clinging to the truth they see and stepping boldly into unknown and untested territories.

Disciples today who espouse openness and connectedness will inevitably experience the vulnerability that comes in their wake. Some decisions will be lonely and their consequence fraught with controversy. There are no certain directions when one is on pilgrimage. Even the detours and the delays, the mistakes and the misfortunes, can be integrated, if the vision guides. We cannot be genuine pilgrims if the maps are clearly marked and the destination is ensured. We will of necessity anticipate the desert and the gathering clouds over Jerusalem, but our journey remains one of hope and of celebration. For it is the Spirit who breaks into our enclosures and calls us forth from our tombs.

"Every call of the Holy Spirit begins with a revelation of the bankruptcy of one's present, habitual mode of life, its tendency towards the death of one's spirit. That moment of awakening inevitably has to be a moment of anguish, of agony and of repentance, because it is only from the pain of awakening to the contradictions in one's life that the energy to change arises."[4] And so a woman from the suburbs of Milwaukee finds herself on a new path. Joyce Henry, two years short of obtaining profit-sharing status in the firm that employed her, left her job to restore and manage a shelter for homeless men in the inner city. And so a group of women in Southern Ireland have resolved to support one another in their ecumenical pilgrimage. And so a woman from South India writes: "I will try to sow little seeds of courage and hope in the minds of Indian women. Seeds that are then carefully watered that they might grow into resolute action. The soil I work on has been trampled on, ignored, for centuries. It has been fed with dangerous artificial fertilizers, distorted theological and biblical teachings. It has therefore lost much of its energy... But the seed cannot be suppressed because the soil is naturally fertile."

What are the resources for those who pilgrim thus? Where do risk-takers and visionaries find their nourishment and sustenance? Paradoxically, where they have always been found: in the deep valid roots of our traditions, in the stories and companionship of fellow pilgrims, in living testimonies from the world church. One of our young friends, alienated from the institutional church, a peace activist and a feminist, has told us of her longing to pray, to meditate, to be centred. Brought up in a middle-class religious home, she is rediscovering the gospels as a source of truth and wholeness. The scriptures speak to us afresh when we engage with them out of our quest, our struggle, our concrete experience. The promise is renewed: of the covenant, of the Magnificat, of the Beatitudes, of Jesus' farewell discourse. The invitation is renewed: to love our neighbour as ourselves, to forgive our enemies, to set our hearts on the pilgrimage, to become the grain of wheat. The parables are unfolding in our midst: the Good Samaritan, the prodigal son, the workers in the vineyard, the Pharisee and the publican, the widow's mite, Dives and Lazarus. "I contend that in a divided Christianity, instead of reading the Bible to assure ourselves that we are right, we would do better to read it to discover where we have not been listening."[5]

And the witness is there, in the saints and mystics, the holy ones, of our traditions. Why are we today rereading so avidly Meister Eckhart and Hildegard of Bingen, Julian of Norwich and John of the Cross? The wholeness and humanness of Celtic spirituality is restated in the liturgies of Iona and Corrymeela. The Franciscan movement finds rebirth in small communities in the East End of London, in Calcutta, in Vezalay, France. The Stations of the Cross, re-enacted in San Antonio, opened up, for those who participated, a new confrontation with the world's pain and suffering.

We have discovered, in our contacts with diverse groups, that it is the sharing of stories, the breaking of the bread of our experience, that nourishes. Women in particular are using this method to unlock the depths of pain and of longing, and to balance the cerebral with a holistic approach. We recognize the value of poetry, of journal-writing, of films and novels, in describing and enriching our pilgrimage. Stories from the world church are vitally relevant to discipleship. But not simply travellers' tales. It is the unsung, unwritten stories of those who faithfully struggle in difficult situations that need to be gathered and offered, to inspire and energize other local Christians.

We speak again of people's longing for something bigger, something with which they identify and belong, that enlarges their perspective and deepens their obedience. We have spoken of our tendency as Christians, as theologians, as God-talkers, to try to "capture" God, to limit and restrict God, to create a God who suits our schemes, our coherent philosophies, our small spirits. We are being called today, through diverse voices — women, poets, third-world Christians, naturalists and scientists, young disciples — to release God. It is a time for imagination and for re-visioning, time to allow God to reveal the many faces and activities that might captivate and conquer our cautious, narrow, inadequate minds and hearts. God is bigger than, more generous than, more embracing than, we can ask or imagine. God is the God of life, not of laws and institutions. God is the God of Abraham and Sarah, of Isaac and Rebecca, of Jacob and Rachel, the God of the covenant, of liberation and of promise. God is the persistent God who struggles with Jacob, over-whelms Job, seduces Jeremiah. God is the God who brings back the exiles, who rebuilds ancient walls, who gathers the people. God is the imaginative God who opens up ways in the wilder-ness and rivers in the desert. God is the just God who hears the cry of the poor and who overthrows the plots of the powerful. God is the tender God on whose hand is inscribed each one's name, who stoops down to guide Ephraim's steps, who carries the lambs and the ewes. God is the Father of Jesus Christ, who offers the experience of communion, of union, to all who are open. This is the God Jesus revealed in the parables, in the kingdom stories, in his encounters with Nicodemus and the Samaritan woman. Our discipleship is within this ambience and this association.

Therefore our questions and our obedience must follow this route of openness, of inclusiveness, of vulnerability, of compassion. It is a *spirit* that we are after, a spirit of freedom and of mercy, of hope and of renewal. Of course we respect the interpretations of the scriptures that have been handed down to us, but we insist as well in returning to tap these wells afresh. Of course we recognize the importance of doctrine and its pivotal place in the life of our churches, but we recognize as well the Spirit that calls us, not to limit God or theology or discipleship to doctrinal formulas, but to release us into the world of community-discernment, of personal and communal response.

We could at this point try to name some of the directions our discipleship together might follow. Some would say: an ecumenical order. One friend of ours has for many years dreamed of an ecumenical order, a structured way of bonding ourselves together. "It is possible to 'go it alone' and doggedly live out an ecumenical life-style of one's own. This is difficult to do and often peters out in disillusionment and despair. The value of an Order is that we share a common journey. We are carried by others when we are low; sometimes our own hope inspires hope in others and when the going gets tough we are fortified by each other's presence. Membership of (this) Order (would be) through the taking of a vow. An Order takes discipleship seriously and is resolute and demanding. An Order does not turn its back on the church but lives as a stream within it."[6]

A covenanting for justice, peace and the integrity of creation is the goal set for the 1990 worldwide gathering at Seoul. What will all the talk of the JPIC covenanting result in? Will those concerns be taken to the ends of the earth, to every congregation and community and become an integral dimension of the preaching and practising of the gospel?

New vows, say some, or a new threefold Franciscan cord. The moment when the Franciscan movement was born was a moment when many were searching for something authentic. Out of the mushroom growth of that time two streams have survived: the Waldensians and the Franciscans. What movements of our time are deep enough to endure and to carry life forward?

These and other steps *might* be taken. But only, we pray, if they embody a *spirit* of openness, connectedness and incarnated commitment. One thing we feel sure of is that no mere restructuring can elicit this spirit. At this time of writing, the BCC has courageously given up its old life that a new one may be born with wider representation (most particularly including RCs). Similarly, the WCC is once again attempting to restructure itself. A Scottish Presbyterian writes critically:

> The current proposals are an attempt to prevent *deep* change; they are tinkering with trivialities. There are some of us who believe that the whole of the church today in the West has to undergo a perestroika, as deep as that which is shaking society within the Soviet Union and Eastern Europe, that the structures that may have served the church fairly well over the last two hundred years are no longer adequate and have to go. The congregational nature of the church puts faith in buildings, presbyteries, synods and committees, which is top-heavy. Instead of the current BCC proposals, we need an era of holy anarchy, a loosening up to a way of the Spirit which will spread through the church by dissidence, questioning, experimentations, and facing the hard questions about creation and suffering.

A second conviction we have is that the Spirit will guide and direct our discipleship if we dare to welcome one another into our church families, to our eucharistic feasts, to engage with one another in imagining and envisioning a round-table church. When we have liberated each other from our inability to grieve, from our fear to imagine, from our delusions of power, from our seductions to affluence and independence, from our complexes regarding loyalty and tradition, from our blindness to the realities around us, who knows what will be possible? "See the fields white and ready for harvesting."

Perhaps we will enter into the spirit of openness. "It will not be so among you," Jesus said, this clinging to the way of the world's institutions, the way of control and domination. Rather, events around us and our common journey prompt us to give each other a say, a job, an encouraging and welcoming word.

They prompt us to free one another to discover our rightful citizenship in the realm of God, to become the places where change and generosity and exchange are born. In the words of Bishop Holloway of Edinburgh: "God in his patience has offered us another cup and invited us to another baptism. If we drink that cup and submit to that baptism, we'll be called to abandon control over our separate futures and submit them to the mind of Christ who does not hold on to power, but empties himself of it and takes only the form of a servant."[7]

"We have received not the spirit of the world, but the Spirit which is from God, that we might understand the gifts bestowed on us by God" (1 Cor. 2:12). We will become receptive to the cries, the pain, the yearning for change, that is coming from so many segments of the Christian community. We will become receptive to the anomalies and diversities that are represented in our questions and our search. No worldly wisdom can bring us the discernment we need as we engage with the powers and principalities, as we seek the unity Jesus prayed for. No worldly training can prepare us for the demands that will be made on us if we sincerely open ourselves to the joys and the pain, the glory and the agony, of our world.

"And I, if I be lifted up, will draw all things to myself." All things are within the compass of God's activity and God's concern. Rather than debating who are the ecumenists, who are the reconcilers, who are the architects of unity, we will rejoice in the diversity of gifts and vocations and the unity of our vision. "The great ecumenical vision, as I have understood it," Michael Kinnamon has said, "insists that joyful proclamation of Christ, active struggle for peace and justice, and realization of our oneness in visible eucharistic fellowship are not competing priorities but authentic, complementary, utterly intertwined responses to the one gospel."[8]

Hopefully, we will live more consistently within a *spirit* of our relatedness and of the relatedness of the whole of creation. Sacred events and sacred words can speak to us in a multi-faceted way. "This is my body" includes the universe, the entire scope of creation, the human assembly, the community of Christians, our daily bread, the bread of the eucharist. "Do this in memory of me" means: release your life and energies for the good of others, become transforming agents of your own society, recognize the relationship between the way you live and the worship you offer, gather in my name, become bread broken and wine poured out.

We will begin to see the patterns of eternity within the rhythms of our own lives: sorrow and joy, death and life, giving and receiving, macrocosm and microcosm, universal and particular, the refusal of exchange that is sin and the flow of exchange that is love. And the patterns of hope: seeds planted, risks taken, encounters blessed, boundaries pushed back, categories broken open. And the oneness of the common cloth of humanity: altar and street, home and distant lands, money and exchange. "The human face of God", John Pobee writes, "is a key to a vibrant, coherent and vital theology."[9]

We need no longer separate our discipleship from our human existence. We will live in the context of the gospel, do our theology in the context of our times, pray out of the struggles we face, and struggle because of the prayer that enlarges us. Our experience will be relevant to our faith, our common stories the parables of our time, our relationships and encounters the place where we meet God. Our churches and our ecumenical organizations will be expressions of our common beliefs, but our faith and our ecumenical commitments will not be defined by and contained therein. Theology from above and theology from below will complement and critique each other. Pluralism will not be inconsistent with fidelity. Diversity will be a blessing even when it challenges our own views. The people of God will be more consciously a tent-people, sojourners, a pilgrim band.

Nothing is real which is not earthed. The disciple is not greater than the master, nor the messenger than the one who sends. Jesus marked the way for us, by naming the blocks in his own context: legalism, hypocrisy, narrow-mindedness, self-righteousness. By daring to open doors that were locked and sealed: contacts with Samaritans, women as disciples, friendships with sinners. By countering questions and prescriptions with his own questions and freedoms. By refusing to carry the clutter and the baggage of human institutions. By declaring his true heritage: the Father and I are one. As you have sent me, so I send them.

Our task is to live in that *spirit*, to clear the way and to constantly clear the way. We know some of the blocks that hem

64

us in. We know some of the doors upon which we have knocked in vain. We know some of the prescriptions that have brought, not life, but death. We know our own clutter and baggage. And we know our calling. It all depends on clearing the way. Then we can say: Come, Holy Spirit, recreate us. Come, Holy Spirit, renew the face of the earth.

NOTES

1 Walter Brueggemann, *The Prophetic Imagination*, Philadelphia, Fortress, 1978, p.45.
2 We should do together all that can be done together, and do separately only that which must be done separately.
3 Gwen Cashmore, "A Report on the Ecumenical Situation in Norfolk and Suffolk", April 1989, p.8.
4 Donald Nicholl, *The Tablet*, 21 October 1989, p.1208.
5 Raymond Brown, *One in Christ*, No. 2, 1989, pp.167-68.
6 Aled Davies, "An Ecumenical Religious Order", *One for Christian Renewal*, 1989, No. 2.
7 In a sermon at the BCC assembly, Glasgow, March 1989.
8 Michael Kinnamon, *Ecumenical Press Service*, 1-7 October 1989.
9 John Pobee, *One World*, October 1989, p.22.